W9-AGT-382

Leadership
Lessons For Life

Leadership
Lessons For Life

Alabama
High School Football Coaches
Favorite Quotations & Inspirational Stories

by David H. White, Jr.

BrookSport •2004

We would like to thank the following newspapers for granting permission to use photographs from their archives to make this book possible — The Birmingham Post-Herald, The Birmingham News, The Decatur Daily, The Auburn Opelika News, The Huntsville Times, *and* The Florence Times Daily.

We would also like to thank the following photographers for granting permission to use their photographs for the publication of this book — Seth Laubinger, Bob Ealun, James L. Yates, Todd Van Emst, and Glenn Peppers.

If you are interested in using Leadership Lessons for Life *for fundraising purposes or for corporate gifts, please email us at SpecialSales@BrookSport.com.*

To Jimmy Webb,
who has been a second father to me.

CONTENTS

FOREWORD

Excellence is to do a common thing in an uncommon way.

Booker T. Washington

BY DAN WASHBURN

EXECUTIVE DIRECTOR OF THE ALABAMA
HIGH SCHOOL ATHLETICS ASSOCIATION

The ultimate satisfaction for the high school coach is to learn that his or her former players are still giving their level best every day, raising happy and caring families, making positive contributions to communities all across the nation. These are the very real, the very tangible rewards that coaches reflect upon and appreciate after having spent so many years mentoring young men and women on the playing field.

It is as true today as it was in my youth—leadership skills often begin with an influential high school coach. I played for three different coaches in high school, Chick Pilkington, Herman "Buck" Watson, and Guy Wilkes. Each of these individuals had a great influence on my life. Coach Watson, for example, who played college football at Vanderbilt and pro football with the Green Bay Packers, brought a tough, determined outlook to a group of 1950s LaFayette high school kids who had little more than a desire to win. When I was a senior, Coach Wilkes had a great deal to do with making sure that I had the opportunity to sign a scholarship with The University of Chattanooga. It was my only chance at a college education.

We all require mentors in our lives, good examples who will help us walk straight in our later years. I found my first good example in Doug Lockridge, the head coach at Valley High School. When, after five years of service as assistant coach, I left Valley to go to Lanett, Doug gave me a very valuable piece of simple advice. "If you can recognize ability and put it in the right place at the right time, you'll win football games."

Sportswriter David White has done a truly remarkable job of reaching out to all corners of Alabama. Understandably, conflicts in scheduling and deadline pressures made it impossible for David to include all the great Alabama sports leaders. Bubba Scott, for example, former executive director of the Alabama High School Athletics Association from 1965-1990, successfully shepherded the athletics association through the troubled times of integration. He brought girls athletics to a point where it now thrives. His great vision, integrity, and disciplined leadership remain unparalleled.

David White has done a common thing in an uncommon way. He has organized timeless principles into an original format, and the result is a literary expression of the simple characteristics of hard work, honesty, dependability, integrity—the generous dividends we benefit from thanks to the selfless efforts of the humble high school coach.

INTRODUCTION

Leadership is a potent combination of
strategy and character, but if you must be
without one, be without strategy.

General H. Norman Schwarzkopf

BY DAVID H. WHITE, JR.

After many hours of discussion and brainstorming with a bookselling friend of mine, I decided to pursue this writing project featuring Alabama's high school football coaches. Having been in the sports reporting business for almost 20 years, not only did I then, as I do now, believe in the merits of the subject, but, as a native of Alabama, I also hold a deep admiration for the people behind the subject—the high school football coaches and the many civic and business leaders these coaches have helped to shape and inspire over the years.

I decided I wanted to create a book that would celebrate the Alabama high school football coaching profession and the extraordinary job they have accomplished as teachers over the years.

First, I had to assemble hundreds of quotations that would add value to their work, notable quotes of men and women throughout history, quotes that embody the timeless values so frequently called upon as we make our way through the complications of our lives.

The editorial challenge would be to isolate a readable selection of quotes that, when strung together, would create their own compelling, dynamic force without being hackneyed or clichéd. The quotes had to be perfectly suited and seamlessly appropriate to the subject.

With the help of my editor, I created a thematic outline, and arranged and cataloged over 2,500 possible quotations taken from over 35 books as well as from other sources. I chose quotations I believed would most likely resonate with coaches as well as with my friends and writing colleagues.

Eventually, after completing the interviews of the coaches, I would then narrow down the initial selection to include only those quotations that best reflected and reinforced the values emphasized by the coaches in the book. I wanted the quotes to adequately reflect the challenges Alabama's young men continue to confront in today's competitive environment of high school football.

Next, I had to survey the incredible pool of talented Alabama football coaches and arrange to contact and interview each of them. This was not going to be an easy task, especially considering that the interviews would have to be taken during football season and I would have to travel all over the state. Nonetheless, many of these coaches were able to adjust to my tight scheduling deadlines.

As I sifted through the stories of these highly regarded football coaches, I quickly came to realize just how important they are to the young men they teach. I was determined and convinced that the book should, first and foremost, focus on education. Although these coaches take teaching their sport very seriously, many of them teach in the classroom as well. During the course of my travels, for example, a secretary in Prattville Coach Bill Clark's office told me that Spence McCracken, now head football coach at Opelika, was one of the best teachers she ever had in history. And, in case you aren't familiar with him, McCracken is a pretty fair football coach, having won three Class 6A state titles.

The main message that kept coming through in my interviews was the coach's true concern for the best interests of his players. Each coach honestly and sincerely expressed his commitment to making his players better as people. Sure, they easily remembered their team's great moments, and, sure, they remembered which player or players made key plays in a game. But they most happily remembered the player who, at the end of the season, had learned from the season's experience and had gained confidence from the competition.

There is no doubt that these men are highly competitive. Winning on Friday nights is priority one. But these coaches aren't ashamed to express their concern for their football players. The best ones care where their players are going to be in their respective futures. They mainly want these young players to succeed as people in society.

Responsible physical education and character building, that's really what these coaches are all about. They're like second fathers, and, in some cases, they're the only father figure in these young men's lives.

Coaches sure don't love every minute of their jobs. This is not a Pollyanna story. Frankly, there is a lot more to the job than practice and games. They issue equipment, keep up with grades, line the field, cut the grass. Much of the work is just, well, work. Still the goal of shaping young men and teaching them about football and life keeps these coaches motivated and passionate about their careers.

Alabama has some of the best high school football coaches in the country. Year after year the best teams in the state can play with anybody nationally. Look at Hoover High School, which won state titles in 2000, 2002, and 2003. They played one of the top teams in the country, Evangel Christian of Louisiana, and beat them.

Retired coaches whom I talked to looked back on their practices and many said they were tougher than some of the college football practices that their former players eventually faced. The hard work paid off many times for the coaches who worked their players to the limits of their capabilities. A great example is Robert Herring, whose teams were known for their mental and physical toughness. He coached at Jones Valley in Birmingham from 1966-1972, which at the time, he believes, was the "greatest high school football place in the South." Herring's intense work ethic paid off as he took Oxford High School to state titles in 1988, 1989, and 1993, and has won over 260 games in his career. He is still coaching in Newnan, Georgia.

Coaching, in many ways, is a selfless occupation. These coaches have met the many challenges that come with being football coach at a high school in a community that eats and breathes the sport. They had to persevere through the tough losing seasons and keep their players optimistic that they could get better despite the malaise that losing can cause. They also had to be able to manage the winning, keeping their players focused on the one-game-at-a-time approach.

To coaches, it's a matter of instilling that esprit de corps mentality that is found in the military. They continually emphasize the unit, the oneness necessary to reach team goals not individual goals. They have to deal with egos both in their players and their coaching staffs and keep up respect and discipline.

Our high school coaches have proven to be effective leaders and educators, putting important life lessons learned on the field of competition to work for our communities. It's teaching in its purest form and there is nothing more exciting than a Friday night playoff game in high school football.

Each of these coaches gets an A+ for their faithful communication of important principles that might not otherwise have been learned in the classroom, principles that can only be learned in the course of intense action, on and off the field of competition.

Principles that have stood the test of time.

BELIEVE

Trust men and they will be true to you,
treat them greatly, and they will show
themselves great.

Ralph Waldo Emerson

1

Believe in your coach, your team, and yourself.

The coaches in this chapter offer real-life, hard-won perspectives on the concept of belief as it applies on the football field. The practical results of such belief—trusting in your coach and in your teammates, taking reasonable risks and facing challenges with courage—can also be read, in a broader context, as creating the foundation for success itself. Belief, these coaches suggest, is fundamental to competition. It is a prerequisite to leadership. It is where winning begins and losing ends.

There are countless high school football coaches who, at one time or the other, have had to make difficult decisions on the field of play, decisions that may have proved unpopular with the fans. The coaches on these pages, however, have successfully navigated the shoals of public opinion by focusing not on "winning" but rather on player development—first, by getting their players to buy into the fact that they can win, and, second, by getting them to trust that this team and this coaching staff offer the best opportunity for winning.

Effective coaches regularly go beyond the call of duty. Such coaches understand the impact and the influence they have on a player's life. They see the player's potential not merely as an asset to the team, but, more importantly, as a vital and contributing member of society. Alabama high school coaches continue to shoulder much of the responsibility of bringing out competitive potential in their players and putting that competitiveness to work.

As young men develop into football players, whether they come from the inner city or from a wealthy suburb, they start to appreciate the significance of teamwork. They learn to trust and believe in others. This practical education flows over into all areas of their lives. A good coach will emphasize positive values and beliefs. A great coach will bring out these qualities in a young man's life and actions.

To the coaches that follow, it's all about changing lives. Football may start out on the playing field but it culminates in a player's belief in himself and in a positive attitude toward life and to those around him.

The secret of getting ahead is getting started.

Mark Twain

If you don't believe you can win, it's a sure thing you won't.

Bear Bryant

Nothing can stop the man with the right mental attitude from achieving his goal. Nothing on Earth can help the man with the wrong attitude.

Thomas Jefferson

The pessimist sees difficulty in every opportunity. The optimist sees opportunity in every difficulty.

Winston Churchill

What we are born with is God's gift to us. What we do with it is our gift to God.

Source Unknown

Never let the clock run out on hope

RON NELSON

Ron Nelson has been a coach for 26 years, all of them at Central Phenix City High School. He coached the junior high for two years before taking on the offensive coordinator role for the Red Devils. He served in that position for 18 years and was, by all accounts, a significant factor in Central's state championship season in 1993.

As head coach for over six years, Nelson has compiled a 43-14 record and has taken his young men to the Alabama high school playoffs every year.

"Believe in your coaches, believe in your teammates, and believe in yourself," says **Coach Nelson**. "If you believe in those three things, you have a chance to make yourself better."

It has been Nelson's experience that it's usually not too difficult to make players believe in themselves. The real challenge for any football coach, he says, is to get them to believe in their teammates and to believe that their coaches have put them in the right position at the right moment. "It's really pretty simple. If you fail at either of those two objectives, you'll never be successful," says Nelson.

Nelson remembers the Red Devils' 1993 quarterfinal playoff game against Benjamin Russell. Nelson says it stands as a superb example of a team trusting in each other and the coaching staff. "At the time I was the offensive coordinator under Wayne Trawick," says Nelson.

The game was tied 0-0 in the fourth quarter in a driving rainstorm.

Benjamin Russell had the ball first-and-goal at the five-yard line. The Red Devils defense held firm, stopping Benjamin Russell on three consecutive downs. On fourth and goal at the two, Adrian Lyles, now an assistant coach at Central, made "one of the greatest hits I've ever seen," says Nelson. Lyles had frustrated the opposition with about six minutes left.

Central proceeded to drive the ball to the Benjamin Russell 40. "A lot of people thought we would run out the clock," Nelson says. "I called time-out and the linemen looked at me like I was crazy."

Nelson called a play-action pass. Quarterback Griff Gordy hooked up with tight end Mark Holland, who ran the ball to the one. The Red Devils punched it in on the next play and won the game 7-0.

"The coaching staff believed in the players' ability to make it happen," Nelson says.

"If the players, in turn, hadn't believed in the call, and in their teammates' ability to execute properly, it would never have worked."

I'm sorry but we can't use you.

Pittsburgh Steelers Coach to Johnny Unitas in 1955.

You can't control what others
think about you.

Vince Lombardi

A man would do nothing if he waited until
he could do it so well that no one could
find fault.

John Henry Cardinal Newman

What matters is not the size of the dog
in the fight, but the size of the fight
in the dog.

Dwight D. Eisenhower

How you respond to the challenge in
the second half will determine what you
become after the game.

Lou Holtz

A little dog looks bigger if he's bitin' at
your heels

JAMIE RIGGS

In 15 years as head coach at T. R. Miller in Brewton, Jamie Riggs has earned the reputation as one of the premier high school coaches in the state. He has tallied a career record of 197-53 (79 percent) with four state championships, and his teams have advanced to the state semi-finals on four other occasions.

Although Riggs has achieved his results with a football program that is steeped in tradition (since 1964, T. R. Miller has experienced only two losing seasons), his personal impact on the Miller program is unquestioned. A native of Brewton, he played tailback for the Tigers from 1970 to 1973 and he was an assistant on the T. R. Miller state championship team of 1984.

"They had a terrific team, and we were decimated by injuries," **Coach Riggs** recalls. It was, he says, his favorite game as head coach, the 1997 regular season shootout with W. S. Neal, Miller's longtime rival just down the road.

"We were out of running backs. We were forced to start a sophomore wide receiver at tailback. I don't think a single fan thought we were going to win that game. Truth is we really hadn't ever been an underdog, and that week we were sure enough the underdog."

Riggs says he had a good talk with the team on Tuesday before the game. 'Nobody thinks you're going to win this game,' he told them after practice, 'but, let me tell you, we're going to win this game.'

The Tigers seemed relaxed and confident entering the game. "I told my players that if the game was close at halftime, they would be upset because they think they're going to beat us by 30," says Riggs.

Riggs' players kept it close, and they won it. The strong heart of tradition overcame the superior first-team talent of the other side.

Riggs says his greatest desire is that each of his players will take with them the motivation to succeed. "I would like for them to leave this program with the self-image they have done something tough," he says. "I want them to have developed a drive and a belief in themselves."

Jamie Riggs has developed a football tradition that is one of the most powerful in Alabama. Riggs attributes his success to a dedicated coaching staff, players with tremendous heart, and a community that unequivocally believes the Tigers have a chance to win every Friday night.

Riggs says that many of his former players may not have understood why they were working so hard when they played for him. "But," he says, "to a man, they appreciate it now."

LEADERSHIP

Whether you think you can or whether
you think you can't ... you're absolutely
right!

Henry Ford

Courage is rightly considered the foremost
of the virtues for on it all others depend.

Winston Churchill

Don't let the fear of striking out
hold you back.

Babe Ruth

If you keep on saying things are going
to be bad, you have a good chance of
becoming a prophet.

Isaac Bashevis Singer

Get in the game. No one is impressed with
the won-loss record of the referee.

John H. Holcolm

Stand up to your competition and you've got him where you want him

JACKIE O'NEAL

Jackie O'Neal, a graduate of Reeltown, returned home to coach right after college. He has now been with the Rebels for 26 years, 16 as the head coach. O'Neal started out working for the legendary Duane Webster, from 1978 to 1987. (Webster won 208 games at Reeltown, taking the Class 2A state championship in 1987, his last year.)

O'Neal became head coach in 1988 and his record is 137-67, averaging between eight and nine wins a year. His 1990 team reached the Class 2A semifinals, and the 1991 and 1992 teams both reached the state championship game. His 2000 team reached the Class 1A state championship game. After pounding on the door for 13 years, Reeltown won the state in 2001 with a 14-1 record.

"They thought we didn't have a chance," **Coach O'Neal** remembers. Flomaton had come into the game undefeated and they had dominated the first half, taking their 20-7 lead over Reeltown into the locker room at halftime.

"My kids had their heads dropping," O'Neal says. "They had played as hard as they could and nothing was working." O'Neal decided he would take a Bear Bryant approach in his halftime talk. "I told them we've got them where we want them. The kids thought I had lost my mind."

O'Neal then proceeded, in great detail, to tell his players that they would get the ball on their own 20 to open the second half. They would drive it 80 yards to score. It would take 15 plays. That would cut the lead to 20-14. Then, he said, the defense would stop Flomaton and they would punt. The offense would take it 75 yards to score in the fourth quarter and take the lead, 21-20. Finally, he told them the defense would hold and the offense would run out the clock. "If you don't believe it, take off your pads right now."

The Rebels took the ball on their own 20 and went 80 yards in 17 plays. The defense held. The offense got the ball back and drove to the Flomaton four with a minute left in the third quarter. However, on the next play, the Rebels running back took the pitch on a sweep and, instead of staying outside and running for the pylon in the end zone, cut up the middle, was hit, and fumbled. Flomaton recovered and advanced to midfield. "I went out to my defense and told them they were not going to make a liar out of me. They were going to hold."

The Rebels got the ball back at their own 15 with 7:45 left in the game. O'Neal told his offensive coordinator to be ready to make adjustments because "we were not going to punt." The Rebels converted three fourth down situations and scored with 1:37 left in the game.

"You would have thought we had won the state championship." And it's a good bet they all believed they could have on that night.

There is very little difference in people,
but that little difference makes a big
difference. That little difference is attitude.

W. Clement Stone

Nobody holds a good opinion of a man
who has a low opinion of himself.

Anthony Trollop

If you don't believe in yourself, very few
other people will.

Source Unknown

Pessimism never won any battle.

Dwight D. Eisenhower

Believe that you can whip the enemy, and
you have won half the battle.

General J. E. B. Stuart

You gotta believe in the kid who runs
a 5-flat 40 in 4.8

BILL BURGESS

Bill Burgess started out as an assistant football coach in 1963 at Banks High School, working under Shorty White, a legend in the high school ranks. "He taught me how to be organized and how to get the most out of the players," says Burgess.

In 1966 Burgess became head coach at Woodlawn, where he stayed until 1971. In 1971 Burgess went to Oxford High School. In his 14 years at Oxford, he earned a 107-41-3 record (71 percent) and took his teams to the playoffs eight times.

In 1986, Burgess moved to the college level, taking the head coaching job at Jacksonville State University. From 1988 to 1992, Burgess posted a 56-8-1 record and took his teams to three Division 2 national championship games, winning the national title in 1992.

"It's really all about getting the players to believe in the coaches and their system, then getting them to believe in themselves and their capabilities," says **Coach Burgess**.

Burgess and his staff made it a daily priority to reinforce in their players the resolve that they would win on Friday night, no matter who the opponent was. "There were a couple of weeks when I don't believe our players even knew who they were going to play on Friday night," he says. "They would dress out for Monday practice prepared to work hard and get ready for the game. The opponent wasn't really an issue."

Burgess admits that he worked his players hard during practice. "First, we got our kids in shape," he says. "We knew that if we could get them in the weight room and get them stronger we could win."

And he knew for his players to believe in what he was doing, he needed to win games. "We went hard during the week in practice; we wanted to play as hard as we possibly could on Friday nights," Burgess says. "We started to win and the players started believing in us and the system. It was a heckuva lot of fun."

Burgess takes perhaps his greatest pride in having taken kids from the Oxford community and turned them into players who wanted to win for the team and the school and the community. "I loved being around that type of student," he says. "Football's a team sport. I wanted to be around the player who played hard every play."

"A team's potential can't be realized without belief," says Burgess. "Every single effort, every accomplishment in the life of a community starts with faith."

"I think my greatest moments as a coach were when I was on the practice field coaxing and convincing the average kid to play above and beyond his natural ability," Burgess says. "It's all about finding that kid who might be able to run, at best, a 5-flat 40 but truly believes he can run a 4.8."

None are so old as those who have
outlived enthusiasm.

Henry David Thoreau

Everyone who got where he is had to
begin where he was.

Robert Louis Stevenson

Success is never final; failure is never fatal. Courage is the only thing.

Winston Churchill

The person born with a talent they are meant to use will find their greatest happiness in using it.

Johann Wolfgang von Goethe

There is no security on this Earth. Only opportunity.

General Douglas McArthur

Tell a kid he's not any good, that's exactly
how he'll play. Tell a kid he's something
special and he'll perform that way

RONNIE HAUSHALTER

*Ronnie Haushalter coached football at Valley Head and Fyffe High Schools
from 1960 to 1994, with a brief stint at Jacksonville State University for
one year in 1969. During his outstanding career, Haushalter compiled
a 217-142-3 record and took 16 of his teams to the playoffs. He coached
four teams to undefeated regular seasons. He coached High School All-
Americans Charles Carden, who played for Haushalter in 1967 at Valley
Head, and Danny Ridgeway, who played for him at Fyffe in 1970.*

*Haushalter, 68, is retired and living in Fyffe. He was inducted into the
High School Hall of Fame in 1996.*

"We did a lot of hitting," **Coach Haushalter** recalls. "We had a lot of three-on-three drills. Our fourth team players always wore blue, the color of Plainview," he smiles. "Of course, you gotta understand, I never thought too highly of Plainview."

Haushalter made an impact on many football players in his 34 combined years first at Valley Head and then at Fyffe. Four of his players are head coaches today, Brian Mashburn at Sylvania, Paul Bennifield at Fyffe, Tim Cochran at Plainview, and Paul Ellis at Fort Payne.

"Our practices were always tougher than the games," says Haushalter. "I had my players believing that they could beat anyone on a Friday night."

Haushalter's tough approach to practice paid off, producing some terrific football programs, one of his most memorable being the 1986 Fyffe team. "This team was gritty," says Haushalter. "They believed in what we were trying to teach them and they hung tough despite losing their first two games."

In the playoffs, they won their first game and then faced Hazlewood in round two. Hazlewood, a traditional power in Class 2A, was picked to win the state that year. Nobody expected Fyffe to compete with the bigger, stronger, and faster Hazlewood team . . . nobody except, of course, for Haushalter, his assistants, and his players.

"We had played Courtland earlier in the year and we only lost 28-21," Haushalter remembers. "Nobody was able to stay with Courtland and I knew if we could keep it close (with Courtland), we could play with Hazlewood and win."

Haushalter says that he and his players were heckled by the opposing fans before the game. "That was a big mistake," says Haushalter.

The game, played on a rainy, cold night with the temperature in the 30s, was tied 12-12 with three minutes to go and Hazlewood had the ball on the Fyffe eight-yard line with a third and one. "We stopped them both times," Haushalter recalls. "Then, on our winning drive, running back Tim Cochran was something to behold."

"We believed in ourselves and knew we could win," says Haushalter, "but after hearing their fans laughing and carrying on, we knew we couldn't lose." And they didn't.

Act as if you are already a winner and that
will tend to make you win.

Dale Carnegie

When you risk nothing, you risk
everything.

Source Unknown

I'm not going to get it close. I'm going to make it.

Tom Watson

Too many people overvalue what they are not, and undervalue what they are.

Malcolm Forbes

The one that makes you proud is the one who isn't good enough to play, but it means so much to him, he puts so much into it, that he plays anyway.

Bear Bryant

Nobody "looks" like a winner until the score's been added up

BILL BACON

Bill Bacon spent 36 years in the coaching profession, with 27 of those years at Enterprise High School and nine at B. C. Rain. He posted a career record of 242-109-5. He won Class 4A state titles at Enterprise in both 1979 and 1982, when 4A was the top classification.

From 1976 to 1984 his teams went 90-13 (87 percent), averaging 10 wins a season. His teams made the playoffs 16 times. Fifty of his players earned Division One scholarships

A native of Aberdeen, Mississippi, Bacon is now retired and living with his wife in Enterprise. He was inducted into the Alabama High School Hall of Fame in 1999.

"As a younger coach, I'd look at a boy who was small or skinny, and I'd think to myself 'he's going to be swallowed up in his uniform,'" says **Coach Bacon**.

Then there was Richard Bedsole.

"Bedsole completely changed my perspective and my judgment about how to look at talent," says Bacon.

Bedsole came into the Enterprise program his freshman year weighing 90 pounds. "I tried to talk him out of playing," Bacon recalls, shaking his head. "He could not lift the bar, and I tried to get him to become a manager."

Bacon says that Bedsole had an unparalleled belief in himself. He worked with weights and practiced hard every day. It was Bedsole's work ethic and dedication to his coach and teammates that made him a hero in Bacon's eyes. "He just stuck with it and became a player," Bacon says.

Bedsole became a starter for Bacon in 1980 and in 1981, his senior year, he intercepted nine passes at safety. Enterprise finished 11-2 in 1980, losing to Parker in Birmingham in the semifinals on a frozen field. In 1981 they went 8-1, losing to Northview, the eventual state champion. "He was a fabulous kid who wouldn't accept that he couldn't play on the team," Bacon says. "He got real strong for his size and he made both seasons unforgettable for the entire team."

Bedsole was the first of many, many players that Bacon helped to develop. "I coached a lot of players at Enterprise who may not have been gifted with natural talent, but I never cut anybody," he says. "I had learned that there are just too many times when a young man who doesn't 'look' like he would be any good winds up being a real player."

These are the kids whose beliefs have the power to place them among the best players on the team.

Your attitude has a definite effect
on your altitude.

Fisher DeBerry

Don't be afraid to give up the good to go
for the great.

Kenny Rogers

They can because they think they can.

Virgil

The achievement of your goal is assured
the moment you commit yourself to it.

Mack R. Douglas

Don't let anyone else's opinion of you get
you down, because the only opinion that
counts is yours.

Terry Bradshaw

Humble beginnings make for successful endings

E.L. "MOOSE" GODWIN

E. L. "Moose" Godwin spent 26 years coaching at three different high schools, Millry, Flomaton, and Smiths Station, where he spent his final 16 years. Over his football coaching career, Godwin put together a record of 190-82-2, averaging 7.2 wins a year.

Godwin took his 1988 and 1989 Smith's Station's teams to the Class 5A state championship games. In 1990 he took his team to the semifinals.

He was tagged "Moose" in high school because he would ride a Harley Davidson motorcycle to school and his red hair would flip up, and one of his classmates said he looked like a moose. The name stuck.

Godwin, 66, retired in 1991 and was inducted into the Alabama High School Hall of Fame in 2003.

Johnny Frank Edwards played for Smiths Station in the 1970s. "Johnny Frank had been living in several foster homes," remembers **Coach Godwin**, "but he wound up living with his aunt when he moved to Smiths Station."

Godwin, then in his first years as a football coach, says that nobody knew what grade to put Johnny Frank in when he moved to Smith's Station from Columbus, Georgia.

"Nobody knew his age," says Godwin.

School officials decided to put him in the eighth grade, and a couple of years later, he came out for football. According to Godwin, Johnny Frank had never seen a football game before, but "he scored three touchdowns in his first game."

Johnny Frank would have to get rides to and from practice every day. "He never missed one in three years," Godwin says. When Johnny Frank scored a touchdown, Godwin's wife, Toni, would bake him a cake. "Football saved his life. If he hadn't played football there would have been only two people who knew him, his aunt and his welfare worker. Football put him in the spotlight. It gave him a chance."

Then there was Eddie James Thomas, who also played for Godwin in the 1970s. "Eddie James was one of 16 children and had to work nights at the mill in Columbus," says Godwin. Godwin recalls a visit to the young man's house. It was freezing outside and Eddie James had no coat. Godwin gave him his jacket. Eddie James played three years for Godwin. At 6-3, 190, he was, Godwin says, "one of the finest defensive tackles I ever had."

After Godwin held the senior banquet, all the players left the locker room except for Eddie James. Godwin told him he needed to go on home, but Eddie James said he wanted to put on his uniform and wear it home so his parents "could see him in it for the first time."

"All he wanted to do was play high school football," Godwin says. "He had told his family he played football, but his parents had never seen him in uniform."

Both of these boys were special to Godwin and to their community.

43

Nothing is good or bad but that our
thinking makes it so.

William Shakespeare

If you don't stand for something, you'll fall
for anything.

Source Unknown

Do the thing you fear and the death of fear
is certain.

Ralph Waldo Emerson

One man with courage is a majority.

Andrew Jackson

I have learned to use the word impossible
with the greatest of caution.

Wernher von Braun

There is great power in a simply stated challenge

MORRIS HIGGINBOTHAM

Morris Higginbotham coached high school football for 27 years, compiling a 190-73-8 record and winning six state championships. He won his first in 1952 at Walnut Grove. He won his next three at West Blocton in 1953, 1955, and 1956. He also won the state at Enterprise in 1959 and 1960.

He had 24 players from his teams go on to play college football. His three sons, Robert, Steve, and Frank all played for him in high school and all three played college football.

Morris Higginbotham was elected into the Alabama High School Hall of Fame in 1993. He lives with his wife in Trussville.

On the afternoon of Monday, November 18, 1963, **Coach Higginbotham** and his Hueytown Gophers opened the last week of practice to prepare for the season's most significant objective. They were scheduled to play their final game on Friday night against the undefeated Bessemer Bucs. Higginbotham was confident they could win even though Bessemer was exceptionally strong and proud. Higginbotham knew he had to motivate his players. To compound an already difficult assignment, Higginbotham knew his players were well-aware of Bessemer's reputation with the home field advantage.

Game day, Friday, November 22, 1963 arrived. President John F. Kennedy was assassinated.

When the teams heard the tragic news, along with the rest of the world, most activities for the day ceased. Events across the nation were being canceled. It fell to the home team, Bessemer, to decide if the game would be played or not. During the week leading up to the game, the Bessemer coaches and players were supremely confident. The Hueytown game would be a virtual cake walk. Bessemer elected to play the game.

When the Hueytown bus reached the first stop sign on the way to Bessemer, Higginbotham stood up and directed a very simple and clear challenge to his team. "Anybody who doesn't have the guts to play this team should get off the bus right now," he remembers.

The teams battled to a 0-0 tie after three quarters. Hueytown took the ball at their own 20 to start the fourth quarter after Bessemer had punted the ball into the end zone to end the third. The Gophers capped a 17-play, 9:15 minute drive to take the lead 7-0.

Hueytown held on to win it, handing out what was perhaps the season's major upset.

Higginbotham believes that courage is one of the strongest leadership characteristics. "That simple challenge on the bus resonated in the heart of every boy on that team," says Higginbotham, "and they responded with a huge win." He knew the death of a president was bound to have affected their attitudes and concentration.

Higginbotham also understood the power of a simple challenge and the call to courage.

PLAN

Nobody wants to follow somebody who doesn't know where he's going.

Joe Namath

2

Intelligence. Discipline. Commitment. Risk.

The coaches in this chapter offer their reflections on leadership skills they have used over the years to prepare young men for the football field. Rather than stressing the mechanics of a typical practice or reading from the pages of a playbook, however, these coaches have chosen to focus their sights on the big picture. Once again, character comes front and center stage.

A sound game plan is, of course, a prerequisite for success on the field. Scout out the strengths and weaknesses of the opposition, plan the response based on your team's resources and assets, sharpen the plan with preparation and practice, and put the plan in play on Friday night. Every coach must walk down this path. Coaches plan because they must plan; it is an indispensable part of the job.

Not surprisingly, we discover that coaches have very little tolerance for those kids who chronically just go through the motions. Coaches invest far more energy and time in developing those players who are focused on the fundamentals. Running, throwing, catching, blocking, and tackling. Every coach becomes enthusiastic about those kids who are eager to put these skills to work in a winning game plan.

A key trait common to great coaches is their ability to ensure that those around them stick to the game plan once it's in place. The coaches on these pages have mastered the practical realities of instilling in each player the twin objectives of, first, understanding and accepting the game plan, and, second, making the commitment to follow it through.

Of course, being prepared doesn't ensure victory, but it does provide an essential footing for future successes. Teams with superior preparation are able to accept a defeat not just with disappointment but also with dignity and a measure of confidence because they realize they have done their very best. They have followed the team plan and they now know where they must improve to succeed the next time.

Young athletes who follow their coaches' instructions, win or lose, will carry a positive team attitude the rest of their lives. It's a great plan for the future.

In the long run men hit only what they aim at.

Henry David Thoreau

Leadership is the ability to get extraordinary achievement from ordinary people.

Source Unknown

What's important is that one strives to
achieve a goal.

Ronald Reagan

It is not because things are difficult that
we do not dare; it is because we do not
dare that things are difficult.

Seneca

Stay organized and keep things simple.

Bear Bryant

There are times when the best and simplest
plan is not to make the same mistake again

WILLIE CARL MARTIN

*Willie Carl Martin, 53, played high school football at Laurel High School
in Alexander City. He played in college at Northeastern State University
in Oklahoma, where he was teammates with Larry Coker, now the coach
at the University of Miami. His coach was Bud Casey, who coached Bo
Jackson, among others, at Auburn later in his career.*

*Martin has been a coach at Benjamin Russell for 21 years, 18 of those
as an assistant. His first year as head coach, in 2001, he won the Class 5A
state championship.*

*In 2001 and 2002, nine of his players advanced to NCAA Division One
football teams. One of these players went to Harvard, a second went to
Columbia, and a third went to Brown University—all in the prestigious
Ivy League.*

"It was a gut-wrenching ride home," **Coach Martin** says of the bus ride from Legion Field to Alexander City after the 2000 state championship game. The Wildcats had just suffered a devastating loss to Homewood, 41-34, in a fierce contest that lasted a record five overtimes. "We had two or three kids with IVs in their arms. We had to keep our defensive tackle out of the game because he was so dehydrated."

Martin recalls Homewood Coach Bob Newton coming down to talk to his team the next week, telling them they played their hearts out. "That didn't erase the sting of the loss, but it did show what a class act Coach Newton is," Martin says.

Rubin Grant of the Birmingham Post-Herald would write of that game that perhaps they should have been named co-champions.

Martin, defensive coordinator in 2000, took over as head coach in 2001, following the retirement of Phil Lazenby. Lazenby urged Martin to prepare the team with his sights constantly set on the ultimate game. "We were determined that if we made it to the championship that year we were not going to let it happen again," says Martin.

"Every day in practice we'd go five overtimes with the offense against the defense," he says. "Honestly, I was afraid that we were going to injure each other in practice, but that's the way we practiced the rest of the season. Five overtimes." And it worked. "Every week, we would be tackling better and we always had fresh legs," Martin says.

The Wildcats finished the regular season with an 8-2 mark, with one of the losses occurring at the beginning of the season to Homewood. In overtime no less. But the Wildcats got their rematch with Homewood in the state championship game. Quarterback Clay Harrelson ran for 137 yards and linebacker Tyrone Martin made key tackles as the Wildcats won the state championship game 20-13.

Willie Carl Martin, a master of the details, won the Class 5A state championship in 2001 by planning not to make the same mistake again.

If you chase two rabbits, both will escape.

Source Unknown

Just do what you do best.

Red Auerbach

The secret is to work less as individuals and more as a team. I play not my 11 best, but my best 11.

Knute Rockne

Most battles are won before they are fought.

Sun-tzu

It's not the will to win that matters—everyone has that. It's the will to prepare to win that matters.

Bear Bryant

Doing the math will add up to victory

JACK WOOD

Jack Wood is Hewitt-Trussville football. Wood coached the Huskies for 19 years, leading his teams to the playoffs 15 times. From 1990 to 1998, the Huskies won the second-most games in Class 6A behind Robert E. Lee of Montgomery. He has coached such standouts as Jay Barker, Jason Standridge, and Brandon Cox. With such talent under his command, Wood is now considered to have been a master at both the run-oriented and pass-oriented offenses; he would win with either game plan.

The Wetumpka native was inducted into the Alabama High School Hall of Fame in March 2003. Since 1995 the Huskies have played opponents at Jack Wood Stadium.

"It's good to know what's most important in life," says **Coach Wood**. "Nothing makes me happier than to see a player exercise the maturity to distinguish between the important things and the insignificant ones."

Wood coached many great young men in his tenure at Hewitt-Trussville, leading them to success on and off the field. One of his more recent standouts, now a quarterback at Auburn, was Brandon Cox.

"It was Brandon Cox's first game at quarterback for us in 2000," Wood says. "He was a junior."

Hewitt-Trussville was on the road going to Huntsville to play Bob Jones High School and Wood was sitting on the front right side of the bus as always. "I'm superstitious like that," he laughs.

Wood prides himself on having been a detail-oriented coach. "One of our rules on an away game was that the players couldn't talk on the bus ride up," says Wood, who believes his players performed better when they relaxed and didn't allow themselves to get distracted by idle chatter. "My assistant, Marty Rozell, was sitting across the aisle from me. I told Marty that I was going to walk to the back of the bus and make sure the players weren't up to no good." On the way back, Wood observed his players with headphones on, listening to music. Some were reading Sports Illustrated, others were sleeping. "

"Then I see Brandon doing his algebra II homework." Wood could hardly believe it. "This is his first game as a starter and he is doing his algebra II homework," recalls Wood.

"We won the game 24-3, and Brandon threw three touchdowns," says Wood. It was Brandon Cox's commitment to learning, planning for his future, and not just winning the game, that provided Coach Wood with a lasting impression.

That bus trip to Huntsville offered Wood an optimistic outlook on the next generation. "It gave me a little perspective that I didn't have before," says Wood.

Never tell people how to do things. Tell them what to do and they will surprise you with their ingenuity.

General George S. Patton

Beware of the man who won't be bothered with details.

William Feather

Spectacular achievements are always preceded by unspectacular preparation.

Roger Staubach

Imagination rules the world.

Napoleon

There are no bad soldiers under a good general.

Source Unknown

Plan on doing the right thing, right now

WALDON TUCKER

Waldon Tucker has done a lot of winning in his 34-year career as a head football coach. He has won more than 250 games and has won two state championships, one at Gordo (1980, Class 2A) and one at Fayette County (1996, Class 4A). He took his 2000 team to the Class 4A state championship game. The 55-year old coach took four consecutive teams to the semifinals from 1989 to 1992.

He has over 20 years at Fayette County, where football remains king in town. "We pride ourselves in playing good people and getting good gates on Friday nights," Tucker says.

"Coaching is a calling, not a profession," says **Coach Tucker**. "When players are coached on how to live their lives, they invariably become better football players."

One look at his career record shows that Tucker is a winner. Yet perhaps the most telling feature to his leadership style is that he seldom chooses to emphasize winning on the practice field. He focuses on character as key to his game plan.

"Character makes a huge difference in my kids," says Tucker. He says that whenever he has a kid with a lot of character, the team stands a better chance of coming out a winner.

"We like to teach our kids more about life than football, and it starts with the way kids act with their elders," Tucker says.

"I want them to go home and tell their mama, daddy, or grandparent that they love 'em and believe in them. I expect to hear, yes sir, no sir, yes ma'am, no ma'am," he says.

Tucker believes it's the player who focuses on the team and not on himself who will make his way in the world. "We're not looking for prima donnas," he says. "We want to surround ourselves with kids who are more concerned about being good people than winning and losing," says Tucker.

He puts much of his thought and effort into developing kids who will plan on being decent to other people in everything they do. Tucker is confident that when he's successful at that, the winning and losing will take care of itself.

"Once again, it's character that ultimately decides whether a player will win or lose," says Tucker. Tucker, a master of offensive football and a master of motivating players, prides himself on being a stand-up guy who looks beyond winning and losing.

When he gets his players to do the right things, on and off the field, he feels he has answered his calling and, what's more, "we're all usually very happy with the results at the end the week," says Tucker.

Dig the well before you are thirsty.

Source Unknown

Chance favors the prepared mind.

Louis Pasteur

People who have all the luck are the ones
who never depend on it.

Bob Ingham

Give a man health and a course to steer,
and he'll never stop to trouble about
whether he's happy or not.

George Bernard Shaw

Teamwork divides the tasks and doubles
the success.

Source Unknown

If you want to be a star, you'd best follow the script

WAYNE TRAWICK

Wayne Trawick has been a head football coach for 43 years and has a 290-145 record. He was inducted into the Alabama High School Hall of Fame in 1996. He coached three undefeated teams at Central Phenix City High School, where he spent 25 years, and had two stretches where his teams were 33-4. He also coached at Cottonwood (five years), Dale County (three years), Andalusia (five years) and Harris County (one year).

Trawick is currently the head coach of Glenwood School in Phenix City, where he has coached for the last four years. Trawick won the Class 6A state championship in 1993.

Forty-three years and still counting.

Ed King and James Joseph played in the NFL. Marco Battle and Vantreise Davis played for Alabama. Jeremiah Castille, a 1982 All-American at Alabama, also became an NFL player. Billy Jackson and Eddie Lowe, who both played at Alabama, were stand-outs in the Canadian Football League.

And all, at one time or another, have followed **Coach Trawick**'s lead into Friday night victories.

Over a remarkable span of years as a winning football coach, Trawick has shuttled no small share of the state's star power into the big leagues. And, he will tell you, he has enjoyed coaching every one of his teams with equal enthusiasm.

Yet, if you press him just hard enough, he won't hesitate too long before confessing that perhaps his favorite was the 1993 Central Phenix City team that won the Class 6A state championship.

"They weren't the most talented group of athletes at Central, but they had a willingness to prepare," Trawick says.

It was their openness to learn each week's game plan that remains most memorable to Trawick. "These boys were bright," says Trawick. "Four of the offensive linemen were in the National Honor Society. Our quarterback, Griff Gordy, was an intelligent young man and we relied on him when times were the toughest."

Trawick cites this inherent eagerness to learn and to follow as perhaps the key for the 1993 team having won it all. "They were ready, willing, and able to put the plan to work every time they hit the football field," Trawick says.

This tremendous desire to follow the plan, to properly execute everything that Trawick and his staff had laid out for them on the drawing board, became contagious. "The attendance at practice was great and the leaders on the team didn't wait for things to happen, but started to make things happen themselves."

"All we did was give them a program with a realistic chance to achieve on the football field," says Trawick. And this is exactly what they did.

Almost by the book.

When one must, one can.

Yiddish Proverb

Fortune befriends the bold.

John Dryden

If everyone is thinking alike, then
somebody isn't thinking.

General George S. Patton

We can't direct the wind but we can
adjust the sails.

Source Unknown

I cannot give you the formula for success,
but what I can give you is the formula for
failure: Try to please everybody.

Herbert Bayard Swope

It's time to hit the brakes when the fog rolls in

TERRY CURTIS

Terry Curtis, head coach at UMS-Wright for five years, has amassed a 137-45 career record (75 percent). His teams won the Class 4A state championship in both 2001 and 2002. He was named Alabama Sports Writers' Coach of the Year in both seasons.

As an assistant at Murphy High School in 1983, Murphy went 15-0 and beat Austin of Decatur in the state championship game. "I thought coaching was going to be a snap," Curtis now laughs. "Then it took me 17 years to win another one."

An all-state football and baseball player at Murphy, Curtis has coached such Alabama greats as Keith McCants, Bill Condon, and current Washington Redskins offensive tackle Chris Samuels.

"It was the worst punishment I could have given them," says **Coach Curtis**.

Curtis has faced many personnel challenges in his 30-year career. "Working with kids, you're never quite sure of what problems they will bring to you the next day," says Curtis.

Sometimes these challenges would prove mildly humorous while at other times the nature of the problems could be gravely serious, demanding swift and severe disciplinary action.

In 2001, UMS had just beaten T.R. Miller in a regular season game. T.R. Miller had come into the game ranked number one in Class 4A. When the fourth quarter ended, UMS was the victor and the stands erupted. It was a huge upset.

The players looked forward to a weekend of celebration. The season's prospects were bright and Curtis anticipated clear, though not easy, sailing ahead.

On Saturday night several of his players were caught drinking. The police called the parents, and Curtis found out about it.

He brought his team together before practice on Monday and asked his players who among them had been drinking. Twenty-two players raised their hands.

Curtis suspended all 22 for the next game against Choctaw County. Despite the pressure he was feeling from the parents to reinstate the players, Curtis stood firm with the disciplinary action.

"It could have worked against us but the kids took it," Curtis says. The coach told the team to never put him in a position like that again.

The players responded to their coach's actions. UMS beat Choctaw Country the next Friday night with many of their starters on the sidelines, out of action.

"Drinking is not a smart idea. There's no place in my plans for a kid who acts irresponsibly in life," says Curtis.

The team learned from their mistake and became a stronger unit. They went on to win every game that season and capture a Class 4A state championship.

Take calculated risks. That is quit different
from being rash.

General George S. Patton

Luck is the residue of design.

Branch Rickey

My plan is to get my 25 guys to play for the name on the front of their uniform and not the one on the back.

Tommy Lasorda

Failing to plan means planning to fail.

Anonymous

Do what you can where you are with what you have.

Theodore Roosevelt

When you plan to deliver a package, a flat tire shouldn't stop you

CURTIS COLEMAN

Curtis Coleman, a coach for 22 years, has raised the bar to the top level at Huffman High School, where he has been the head football coach for over nine years.

In 2000, his Vikings team finished 12-1, making it to the quarterfinals of the Class 6A playoffs.

In 2001, his team finished 13-1, making it to the semifinals before Hoover beat them in a hard-fought game. That same year, Coleman sent 13 players to college on football scholarships. In 2002, his Vikings team finished 6-4 and he sent five more to college on football scholarships. In 2003, he amassed a 7-4 record and sent two players to the college ranks.

There are a lot of things in life you just can't plan on, but when all is said and done, you still have to execute.

A solid game plan allows for the unexpected. It does so not by some magical power of predicting the future but by simply providing a clear path to return to once the dust settles. A good game plan affords a level of confidence that if you fall down you can get back up and forge ahead.

In 1974, **Coach Coleman** played linebacker for Escambia County High School. He played with future University of Alabama standouts Lou Ikner and Don McNeal. His coach was Glen Latham. "I would've run through a concrete wall for that man," says Coleman.

That year, Escambia County played for the Class 3A state championship. Coleman says their team's game plan was built around strength and the players' endurance. "We were proud of our physical game. It was straightforward, in-the-trenches football," says Coleman.

"I remember we're all in the auditorium before the game getting ready to play and I went to sleep with my legs over the back of a chair dreaming about the game," Coleman recalls. "Coach told us it was time to go and I jumped out of the chair." Since his legs had been resting on back of the chair, they had poor circulation. When he got up he collapsed to the floor, spraining both his ankles. Still, that would not be enough to deter him from playing for the state championship. "If I had to go out on crutches, I was going to play," says Coleman.

That's how committed the whole team was to winning.

"We won the game 7-6," says Coleman.

As a coach, Coleman will beat you with great defense and a powerful running game behind some of the biggest lineman in the state. "I expect my teams to be hard-nosed and physical," says Coleman.

It took two bad ankles and a state title to teach him the value of commitment to the plan.

Have a goal. And to reach that goal,
you'd better have a plan. Have a plan that
you believe in so strongly you'll never
compromise.

Bear Bryant

If you don't know where you're going, any
road will get you there.

Thomas Carlisle

What the mind can see, the brain can
achieve.

W. Clement Stone

You have to set the goals that are almost
out of reach. If you set a goal that is
attainable without much work or thought,
you're stuck with something below your
true talent and potential.

Steve Garvey

Often the difference between a successful
person and a failure is not one's better
abilities or ideas, but the courage that
one has to bet on one's ideas, to take a
calculated risk.

Maxwell Maltz

If your life is free of failure, you're not taking enough risks

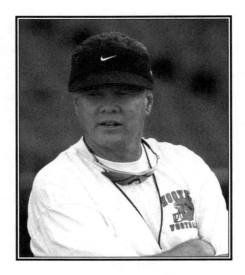

RUSH PROPST

Rush Propst's commitment to coaching has led to tremendous success. In his 15 years as a head coach, Propst has achieved a 130-51 mark, with three state championships at Hoover High School, in 2000, 2002, and 2003.

In summer 2003, Propst lost his mother to cancer. The summer before he had lost one of his players, Victor Hill, who had died on the Bucs practice field before the season opened. Yet Propst and his coaches stuck to their game plan both years and kept their team together and led them to unprecedented second and third state championships in four years in Class 6A.

Propst praises his coaching staff, especially in 2003. "They did the best job a staff has ever done in my 23 years as a coach."

Coach Propst is a man on the move.

Propst has managed his career by constantly taking risks—adjusting to the dynamics of each new situation, adapting his game plan to the talent under his leadership, consistently moving towards greater challenge, because, he says, "that's where the opportunity is."

He started as an assistant coach at Cleburne County High School in 1981, where he spent five years as offensive and defensive coordinator, "lining the fields, cutting the grass, and painting the gym floor."

He moved to Atlanta in 1986, where he served as the defensive coordinator at Cherokee High School.

In 1987, he went to Ashville High School, close to where he'd grown up in Ohatchee. He became head coach in 1989 and led his 1992 team to the state semifinals.

In 1993 he moved to Eufaula, building that program and posting a 10-2 record in 1996.

In 1997 he was named head coach at the new Alma Bryant High School close to Mobile. He took his 1998 team to the state quarterfinals and finished the season 12-1.

He took the Hoover job in 1999 and has taken that program to elite status both in the state and nationally. In one popular sports poll, his teams have been ranked in the top 20 nationally for four years.

Propst believes his penchant for taking chances stemmed from his parents. He was extremely close to them and confided in them throughout his career. His mother, Edna, missed only four games in his 22 years prior to the 2003 season. His dad, Clifford, who died in 1994 of cancer, would regularly urge him 'to take some chances', adding, Propst remembers, 'I don't want you to miss out on any opportunities.'

"My father always wished he had taken more chances in life," says Propst. "He didn't want me to make that same mistake." Propst has taken his parents' lessons to heart and he relishes the prospect of greater challenges each season.

He thrives on the risk.

WORK

Genius is one percent inspiration and ninety-nine percent perspiration.

Thomas A. Edison

3

The coaches in this chapter remind us that there simply are no short cuts for working hard each and every day. It's just old-fashioned, nose-to-the-grindstone sweat and physical labor.

Do what it takes to execute the task, and do it now.

These coaches pride themselves on having been put through the paces when they were players themselves. Each shares a deep respect and affection for the men who trained them and helped them to understand why the work ethic, and the consistency it demands, is so vital to success.

On the practice field, you'll find that these coaches are single-minded about driving tirelessly toward a victory on Friday night. They have developed an unyielding dedication to hard work, and they insist that their players share in that commitment. They have come to realize, through many difficult and challenging years in the profession, that there are no substitutes for the willingness to perform at full-throttle every day.

This intensity of purpose often translates into three-hour practices with physical drills and a lot of running. These coaches point out that their most successful players have exhibited an innate desire to work harder than everyone else around them.

A winning coach must be successful in moving the work ethic from the football field into the classroom, and he must continually strive to set the right example for his players. Players believe in their coaches and naturally follow their leads, and, in doing so, these young men have the opportunity to experience success upon success on Friday nights and in the classroom, and, ultimately, in careers and families and communities around the state. All it takes is hard work.

These Alabama coaches have created great winning traditions for our state's high school football programs. This reputation stands as living proof of what can be accomplished when one pursues a goal with effort and sacrifice.

Whether it is a state championship in football, an A in the classroom, a raise at the office, or the smile on a child's face, effort and sacrifice can be immensely rewarding and satisfying.

3

Nothing will work unless you do.

John Wooden

If I do my full duty, the rest will take care
of itself.

General George S. Patton

Truly, I have never known a really
successful man who deep in his heart did
not understand the discipline
it takes to win.

Vince Lombardi

Well done is better than well said.

Ben Franklin

Good things happen to people who hustle.

*Chuck Noll, Pittsburgh Steelers coach on
Franco Harris' "immaculate reception."*

To develop discipline, one must become a disciple of action

ANDRE ROBINSON

Andre Robinson has the Parker football program on track to become one of the better programs in the state Class 6A. Robinson begins his seventh season at Parker in fall 2004.

Robinson's 2002 team finished 10-2 making it to the second round of the playoffs. His 2003 team proved that Parker is for real with a 8-3 record. Robinson played at Parker from 1973 to 1977 and then went on to play for legendary Coach Eddie Robinson at Grambling. He has been coaching for 20 years under coaches such as Steve Savarese, whom he coached with at Benjamin Russell.

When it comes to developing young football players, **Coach Robinson** focuses on the twin characteristics of discipline and hustle. "Work and hustle will always serve you well," Robinson says, "at work and at home." They are the core values Robinson's players are most likely to carry with them when they move on in life.

Robert Taylor, a 6-3, 235-pound middle linebacker, played for Robinson when he was defensive coordinator for the Parker Thundering Herd in 1997. Robinson says he could easily see the qualities of a winning personality and football player in Taylor.

"Taylor was a great leader," Robinson says. "He kept the players going and playing hard every down." Robinson believes Taylor's enthusiasm at practice and his incredible hustle on game days were responsible for lifting the team's overall performance. "He stands as a great example of what football can do in teaching the values of life," Robinson says.

Robinson is convinced that Taylor's determination and hustle led to a couple of key victories for the Thundering Herd. "In the John Carroll game, in 1997, Taylor picked off two passes and had 18 tackles," Robinson remembers. "Both of us were 4-0 at the time. It had rained all week and that night it was still raining," Robinson says. "One of his pickoffs was thrown behind him. He intercepted it and ran 50 yards for a touchdown. We won the game 35-0."

The other game Robinson remembers was against Hewitt-Trussville when Jason Standridge, a great high school quarterback who now plays for the Tampa Bay baseball franchise, was Hewitt-Trussville's starting quarterback. Taylor recorded 18 tackles; he and his defensive teammates held Standridge to one of ten passing attempts for only seven yards.

"He was a good kid who was a hard-nosed worker on and off the field," Robinson says.

Taylor, who moved on to college at Grambling, was eventually drafted by the Cleveland Browns and is now a graduate assistant football coach at Grambling. "When I played at Grambling," says Robinson, "Coach (Eddie) Robinson stressed going hard all the time, and, if you did, good things were going to happen to you."

A sensible practice and a sound principle.

As I grow older I pay less attention to what men say. I just watch what they do.

Andrew Carnegie

Not now becomes never.

Martin Luther

Big jobs usually go to the men who prove
their ability to outgrow small ones.

Ralph Waldo Emerson

Don't duck the most difficult problems. That
just ensures that the hardest part will be
left when you're most tired. Get the big one
done, and it's all downhill from then on.

Norman Vincent Peale

Always do more than what is required of
you.

General George S. Patton

If you're not working, someone else is

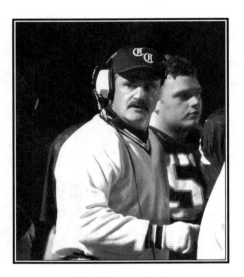

DANNY HORN

Danny Horn has been at Clay County for 15 years, posting a 158-35 record and winning five state championships. His teams from 1994 to 1997 won 55 games in a row, taking three state titles home in Class 2A, in 1994, 1995, and 1996. His 1997 team won their first 11 games before losing in the second round of the playoffs to Luverne.

His 2000 and 2002 teams also won state championships.

Horn is a native of Ashland, Alabama, a town of 1,200. He will tell you that he has a hard time understanding "lazy people."

"They were never complacent or satisfied," **Coach Horn** says of his 1996 senior class. "They continued to work hard every day, every year throughout high school."

They had been part of an incredible 44 straight wins in three years at Clay County.

"As good as they were as sophomores and juniors," and they were very, very good, emphasizes Horn, "they saw every single practice as a way to get better." By the time they were seniors they were dominant.

Horn says the 1996 senior class had desire that the other classes did not seem to have. In 1994, as sophomores, when they experienced the loss of their first game, to Heflin, Horn believes they helped to turn the season around by making significant contributions to wins in the next 14 straight. And, as juniors, in 1995, Horn says they helped in to bring in 15 more wins in a row. Finally, in 1996, as seniors, they would score 613 points, giving up only 42 in 15 games. They posted 11 straight shutouts that year.

"There was pressure on these kids because we had already won two states and there were high expectations," Horn says. "But they met the challenge. They ended up 44-1 in their three years."

Horn's 1994-96 teams bought into his expectations and demands for hard work.

"It's hard to imagine, but many people don't realize how much discipline it takes to play ball," Horn says. "The values we instill in them can last a lifetime. When you get up and go to work even if you don't feel like it, it's like a fourth and one. You've got to step up to the line and call the play."

Horn got that same effort out of his 2000 and 2002 teams, both also winning state championships.

"The 2000 team was a surprise," he said. "And in 2002, they were probably the strongest team I've had." Horn develops such strength by working them in the weight room and running tough practices. Horn believes the benefits can be seen on the field and in the classroom.

"Hard work is a mandate for every one of us and it's a good thing for the entire community," says Horn, "and that's not ever going to change."

You can always outwork the best player in
the world.

Ben Hogan

Chop your own wood, and it will warm
you twice.

Henry Ford

I believe in luck, and I find the harder I
work the more I have of it.

Thomas Jefferson

Pray as if everything depends on God, but
work as if everything depends on you.

Unknown

The harder you work the harder it is to
surrender.

Vince Lombardi

Hard work is hard work

SAMMY QUEEN

While working for Pelham Panthers head coach Rick Rhoades as an offensive specialist, Sammy Queen coached Tyler Watts and Bill Flowers, both of whom became starting players at Alabama and Ole Miss, respectively. Sammy Queen spent six years in this learning role as offensive coordinator before becoming head coach in 2001. Queen is now well on the way to getting Pelham back to where they were in the 1990s as a perennial playoff team.

Before coming to Pelham, Queen coached receivers at UAB when it was a Division III competitor. He was the recruiting coordinator at UAB in his second year.

"There is no substitute for hard work," says **Coach Queen**, who recalls a story about Tyler Watts, one of the state's truly great players in the 1990s. "We were playing Homewood in the 10th game of the season. The winner qualified for the playoffs and the loser went home," remembers Queen. "Tyler just had this tremendous work ethic to go along with his God-given talent."

It was Tyler's senior year and Homewood had scored with three minutes to go. "Homewood went ahead 24-17," Queen says. "They kicked off into the end zone and we were staring at 80 yards. We got the drive going and when we faced a fourth and 10, Tyler got it with a pass to Lane Bearden around the 50 yard line."

The Panthers scored with 50 seconds remaining, but there was a lot of game left.

"We were down 44-37 in the third overtime and scored to make it 44-43," Queen says. "We were going to go for two. Watts was the best player in the state and we had him. Coach Rhoades was willing to put all the stock in the season on one play and one player."

After both teams took timeouts, Queen and Rhoades called the play. "Michael King ran a pick pattern and got open," Queen says. "Tyler found him in the end zone and we won 45-44."

Queen says that perhaps the best team he coached was the 1999 Panthers team that featured standout wide receiver Bill Flowers, who completed a stellar career at wide receiver for Ole Miss, and quarterback Parker Anderson.

The Panthers made it to the third round of the state playoffs where they faced Clay-Chalkville. "We were down 16 points with a little over three minutes to play," Queen remembers. "We scored twice in a minute and a half and went for two both times and made it."

While the Panthers lost to Clay-Chalkville in overtime, on a kick that was partially blocked and just barely made it over the goal post, Queen smiles and says, "We may have been the best team in the state not to have won it."

Watts, Flowers, and Anderson are three of the legendary workhorses on the Panthers' team whose performance stands out because they laid it on the line each and every practice.

91

The truth of the matter is that you always know the right thing to do. The hard part is doing it.

General H. Norman Schwarzkopf

An acre of performance is worth a world of promise.

W. D. Howells

Those who say it can't be done are usually interrupted by others who are doing it.

Joel A. Barker

A wise man will make more opportunities than he finds.

Francis Bacon

Well done is better than well said.

Ben Franklin

A champion's heart is always
in the right place

GERALD GANN

In 38 seasons Gerald Gann has successfully mentored many good players on high school sports teams. Gann coached the Homewood High School football team to state championship game appearances in 1986, 1990, and 1994. He led a Berry baseball team (now Hoover) to the state championship in 1972, and he was an assistant football coach at Berry in 1977 when they won the state. He took one of his girls basketball teams at Berry to the Elite Eight.

Now at John Carroll, Gann is just as motivated to build a winner as he always has been. No matter what happens on the football field Gerald Gann will always teach his players how to win in life.

Having coached young men in team sports for over 38 years, **Coach Gann** will tell you with great confidence and authority that, at the end the day, the true winner is the kid who has learned the value of work on the way to success.

"It's definitely not the kid who has a ton of raw, natural talent but is fundamentally lazy," says Gann. "And it's not the kid who may be street smart and popular with the crowd who wins a lot but doesn't really like to sweat."

"I've mentored many overachievers in my career, particularly on the football field," says Gann, "and there's nothing quite like a kid with heart."

Gann is proud of his accomplishments on the football field, but perhaps his favorite example of an athlete with selfless discipline and heart comes from a different sport altogether.

With Gann as head coach, the Berry Buccaneers baseball team won the state championship in 1972. "There was this player, I'll call him old Richard, who had been shagging balls for the team during batting practice all year and had been supporting his teammates from the bench throughout the season," Gann recalls.

"We were in Montgomery playing the best-of-three game series for the state championship. We had lost the first game Monday night and faced a double-header Tuesday night to decide the series," says Gann. "We won both games for the championship and returned to Birmingham around 2 a.m. We had a league game the next day, and on the bus ride home we were all dog-tired and I realized we didn't have a pitcher without a sore arm."

"Old Richard had been busting his tail all season," Gann says, recalling his decision with great emotion, "and there was no question that he was going to pitch that next day."

It shouldn't be surprising that Gann would ask a player who hadn't played one inning for him to pitch. Gann believes that every player counts if every player has heart.

"It may have been the only game he ever pitched for me, but we won it 5-2," Gann says, "and it goes down in my record book as my favorite victory."

95

God gave us two ends. One to sit on and
one to think with. Success depends on
which one you use; heads you win—tails
you lose.

Source Unknown

It's the job that's never started that takes
the longest to finish.

J. R. R. Tolkien

Just do it.®

Nike

Be content to act and leave the talking to others.

Baltasar Gracian

Action is eloquence.

William Shakespeare

When you don't think it's possible to get
any better, work just a little harder

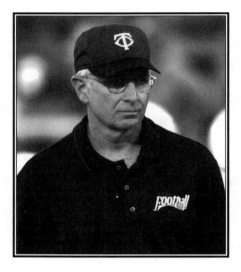

ROBERT HIGGINBOTHAM

*Robert Higginbotham (222-115-3) is one of the deans of active coaches in
the state of Alabama.*

*After a half year at Etowah County, Higginbotham became the
defensive coordinator at Banks High School in 1973, when they won the
state championship title. He next moved to Mountain Brook for three years,
winning the state in 1975, and then to Shades Valley, where he stayed for
the next 23 years.*

*He has just completed his fifth year at Tuscaloosa County High. In his
second year, the team was undefeated and made it to the third round of the
playoffs. In 2002, his team once again made it to the third round, where it
lost to the eventual state champion, Hoover.*

Coach Higginbotham has coached many good football players in his 31 years on the job, but, says Higginbotham, "Major Ogilvie was perhaps my hardest worker."

A Mountain Brook All-State running back and a University of Alabama standout, Ogilvie was the engine that drove the Mountain Brook Spartans to two Class 4A state championships, one in 1975, when 4A was the top state classification and the other in 1976, when Rick Rhoades was at the helm.

Higginbotham had laid a rock solid foundation and had successfully beefed the team up in his first two seasons, 1973 and 1974. The Spartans were well-prepared to take on the 1975 season.

"I knew that if we were going to win we needed one more key player," Higginbotham recalls. "Major came over to our team his junior year in 1975 from Vestavia Hills, and that was just what we needed."

Ogilvie ran for almost 2,000 yards and led the school to its first state title. "Major was the epitome of hard work," Higginbotham says. "If he had a really good day of practice he would still stay after and run on his own. I've never had a player before or since who could make a big play like Major."

Higginbotham believes that because Ogilvie set such a demanding pace during practice and in the games his whole team became more disciplined and focused.

"They were by far and away the most intelligent, mature group of kids I've ever worked with," Higginbotham says. "The hardest thing I had to overcome was getting the kids to believe they could win. We had never beaten Berry before and after we won a knock-down, drag-out game against them, we began to work like we were going to win every game for the rest of the season."

After the 1975 championship season, Higginbotham left Mountain Brook and took over the head coaching position at Shades Valley High in Birmingham. That year he was on the opposing side of his former star player Ogilvie.

"I didn't think it was possible for him to get much better," Higginbotham says, smiling, "but, when I looked up at the scoreboard, I realized he'd never stopped working and, yes, he was a lot better."

Even if you're on the right track you'll get
run over if you just sit there.

Will Rogers

Faith will perform miracles, especially
when you get your hands and feet
involved.

Spencer W. Kimball

He who labors diligently need never
despair; for all things are accomplished by
diligence and labor.

Menander

I believe that any man's life will be
filled with constant and unexpected
encouragement if he makes up his mind
to do his level best each day.

Booker T. Washington

Nothing is work unless you'd rather be
doing something else.

George Hallas

There's no use for no effort

JOEY JONES

In 2003, Joey Jones completed his eighth year as head football coach at Mountain Brook, where he has taken his teams to the state championship game in 1996 and to the semifinals in 2002. His coaching record at Mountain Brook is 87-17 (84 percent). His overall mark is 109-28 (80 percent).

He spent three years as the head coach at Dora High School in the early 1990s. He was selected Coach of the Year by The Birmingham News in 1992, 1996, and 1999. He was chosen as the 2002 Coach of the Year by the Pat Patrick Club, which consists of coaches throughout the state.

"The work ethic was ingrained in me when I was a 7-year-old growing up in Mobile, Alabama," says **Coach Jones**. "I attribute my good work habits to a man named Coach Rogers."

Steve Rogers, a Mobile youth league coach, saw a young Joey Jones running around the house across the street from the football parking lot. It didn't take him long to ask Jones to come out for the team.

"You can bet it wasn't a day or two before I bought some shoulder pads at Kmart," Jones now laughs. "The first time I ran the ball I ran right and left and lost about 30 yards."

Jones says Rogers came into his life at a crucial period. "I had lost my father and Coach Rogers became my role model," Jones says. "We were a close team, and we had a lot of fun. He took us to baseball games. He became a father figure to me."

Jones remembers Rogers calling for bull-in-the-ring drills during practice, where one player gets the ball and another player is called out to tackle him. Coach Rogers also regularly had the team doing "six-inches," a drill in which the players had to lie on their backs and keep their legs exactly six inches off the ground for a minute. They did this, too, knowing that Coach Rogers might step on their stomachs at any time.

"Those were the kinds of drills I needed at the time. Coach Rogers made us mentally tough," says Jones. "And that's why I'm sitting here in this office today."

Jones played for Rogers until he was 12 and it was his extraordinary influence and training that would lead Jones to the University of Alabama and Coach Bear Bryant.

Jones says that although he learned a lot about toughness from the Bear, he still attributes much of his success to his Little League coach. "He's the reason why I tried to have a game face on in every high school and college game that I played in. And that's how I've tried to coach," says Jones.

Jones said while Rogers was a tough leader, "He taught us about what it takes to be good citizens. I'm forever thankful for him."

"The Mountain Brook Spartans may not be known for their size but they are known for their tenacity and their mental toughness," says Jones. "I am most proud of their work ethic."

Once a decision is reached, stop worrying
and start working.

William James

Opportunity is missed by most people
because it is dressed in overalls and looks
like work.

Thomas Edison

You can't build a reputation on what
you're going to do.

Henry Ford

Success is a ladder that cannot be climbed
with your hands in your pockets.

American Proverb

Success usually comes to those who are
too busy to be looking for it.

Henry David Thoreau

There's a close connection between
getting up in the morning and
getting up in the world

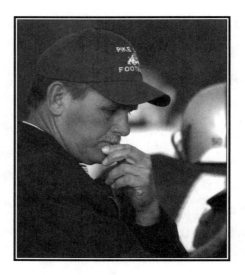

WAYNE GRANT

Wayne Grant, a football coach for 26 years, has earned tremendous respect from his players and his community because of his commitment to excellence. He was an assistant for one year each at Zion Chapel High, Louisville High, and Lowndes Academy before becoming the head coach at Pike County in 1980.

Grant won Class 4A state titles in 1988 and 1989. He then moved to Talledega to be head coach from 1993 to 1998. He returned to Pike County in 1999 and led his 2003 team to the state championship in Class 3A. His last three teams have won 35 games, almost 12 wins a year and reached the semifinals in 2001 and the quarterfinals in 2002.

Coach Grant has made Pike County a special place to play football. The Class 3A school in Brundidge (population 2,000) has produced great football players who have gone on to become highly successful in other walks of life.

The 2003 season serves as a great object lesson, showcasing Grant's work ethic and the results that stem from going the extra mile at practice. It was this positive behavior on the practice field that would lead his players in 2003 to perform at the peak of their ability . . . and maybe even above their heads.

In their first game against Region 1 rival T.R. Miller in the regular season, Grant witnessed his team exceeding everyone's expectations.

"Miller was ranked No. 1 and they were the defending state champions," he says. "We were playing at their place and they had 72 players and we had 25. It was a two-hour road trip. They went up by one point with 67 seconds left. We received the kickoff, ran four plays and scored. It took special athletes to pull that off. I knew the players were going to go on to win the championship after that."

Grant says Chris Nickson, his quarterback in 2003, who was named Mr. Football, the top player in the state, was an incredible force of strength and power for the team. "Nickson would have a one-and-a-half hour session within the practice and then pass for an hour after practice," says Grant. "It was hard workers like Nickson who helped us win the state championship."

Grant has established a first-class program. His influence is felt across the county. Grant's approach is to take every day one at a time. "You need to get up every day and do something positive and winning," he says. "The other team has winning players who will outperform you if you don't work at it. You need to work on your job every day that way, too."

"I tell my players, when you turn 18, football will end, but you have 60 more years in society. You need to get along and be a team worker even though nobody asks for your help. You do it because it's your duty."

IMPROVE

The man who makes no mistakes does not usually make anything of himself.

Theodore Roosevelt

4

There is no progress without improvement. That's the word from the coaches in this chapter.

You may believe in yourself and your team, your plan may be right on the mark, and you may have worked well beyond the call of duty, but the coaching job is not truly over until you've created a culture of excellence, engendering the habit of constantly being on the lookout for ways to do it better.

The coaches on the pages to follow have experienced their fair share of losses, but they are happy to report that over the long haul they have learned more from these losses than from their wins. It is through the losses and the disappointments that they were able to discover the lessons which ultimately led to future success.

Some of the coaches in this chapter have had to withstand the harsh sting of criticism from unhappy fans. They stood in the light of negative publicity and responded to the challenge with courage. They were able to steady the team's weekly performance by focusing on the positive goals of competition, encouraging their players to concentrate on improvement. The short-term results of such long-term thinking added victories to the coaches' win columns ... and silenced the naysayers who had counted them out.

Several of the coaches in this chapter had to deal with significant personal matters involving life and death issues. Their challenge was to keep the team focused while at the same time tending to the emotional needs of individual players. Displaying a high level of care and concern in handling these difficulties not only kept the team together, but also led to significant improvements in the team's morale and, not coincidentally, the team's overall performance.

In the end, winning is not on the scoreboard, but in one's ability to learn from mistakes and to improve relationships with others. You show up every day and you just keep on making adjustments, assessing strengths and uncovering weaknesses. We learn from these coaches that, although there is no such thing as perfection, there are truly great rewards in store when we consistently strive to reach it.

4

The best way out of a problem is through it.

Source Unknown

You can never solve a problem with the same kind of thinking that created the problem in the first place.

Albert Einstein

Your net worth to the world is usually determined by what remains after your bad habits are subtracted from your good ones.

Benjamin Franklin

Losing. You must simply study it, learn from it, and try hard not to lose the same way again. Then you must have the self-control to forget about it.

John Wooden

No man is free who is not master of himself.

Epictetus

No one cares how much you know until
they know how much you care

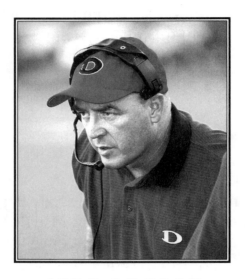

JERE ADCOCK

Jere Adcock, in his 23rd year as a football coach and his ninth as head coach at Decatur, has taken the Red Raiders to the playoffs eight of the 10 years he has been there. He took his 2002 team to the quarterfinals and his 1999 team to the second round, where they lost to eventual state champion Clay-Chalkville.

Prior to coming to Decatur, Adcock was an assistant at Handley High School in Roanoke, Alabama, for eight years where he was part of a highly successful program. Before that he was at Smiths Station and McIntosh High School in Atlanta.

The number one priority of **Coach Adcock** is to build quality relationships with his kids. "Our objective is to try and help them improve themselves as people as well as players," says Adcock.

In typically modest fashion, Adcock attributes the team's success to his players, his coaches, and his community. He's built a perennial playoff program in Class 6A despite not having a large pool of players that other schools in the classification have.

"There's a lot of teaching and learning that goes on as a coach, and we've learned that the best thing we can do as coaches is to build relationships with our young men," Adcock says. "The older you get the more you realize that life is all about relationships."

Adcock says that one of the most challenging times in his coaching career was in the 2000 season.

"One of our players had a sister who died on a Friday before one of our games," Adcock says. "The young lady had been battling a rare form of cancer for over two years."

Adcock had to take this young man home. "He was the quarterback of our secondary. He was one of those kids who didn't have to play football," Adcock says. "He was great academically and always seemed to be in the right spot at the right time."

Adcock wanted to provide a support system for the young man. "On that ride home, I realized what our real job is as coaches, that winning is not the most important part of the job. I wanted the football field to become a place where our players would come to learn about themselves, a place where a player could get away from things that troubled him."

Adcock said the young man's family and community were there alongside him all the way.

"He's got a great family," Adcock says. "The people in the community rallied around and it made me realize what a special place Decatur is. He and his family taught me more, I am sure, than I could ever teach them."

"Make no mistake about it, every one of our kids is special," Adcock says. "We really strive to find ways to invest our time in the progress of their lives."

You should never try to be better than someone else, but you should never cease to try to be the best you that you can be.

John Wooden

Do a little more each day than you think you possibly can.

Lowell Thomas

Admit your errors before someone else
exaggerates them.

Andrew Mason, M.D

Being ignorant is not so much a shame as
being unwilling to learn.

Ben Franklin

The only real mistake is the one from
which we learn nothing.

John Powell

Do the right thing. Do it on time.
Do it the best you can

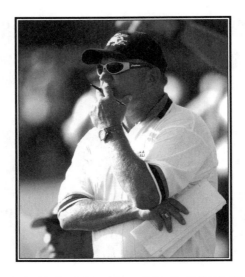

SPENCE McCRACKEN

Spence McCracken's outstanding 24-year high school head coaching career, 234–65 (78 percent), would be enough to convince a lot of coaches that it's time to retire. But McCracken, a 31-year veteran, has not lost an ounce of the enthusiasm that has propelled him to 21 area or region titles and three state championships.

At Montgomery Academy from 1978 to 1983, he won four area titles and one region title. He then went to R.E. Lee High School, his alma mater, where he coached from 1984 to 1994, winning 118 games and losing 25. In those 11 years at Lee he won Class 6A state championships in 1986, 1991, and 1992.

Coach McCracken's understanding of what wins football games has changed over the years.

"I used to think whoever knocked the other fellow in the mouth the most would win the game," McCracken laughs.

"Over time, I discovered that most kids are well coached," continues McCracken. "I learned that the best players and consequently the best teams are the ones who have it between the ears. They know how to listen and are willing to improve. All you have to do as a coach is to keep them ready mentally and make sure they don't get tired of football."

Spence McCracken's first job as a head coach was at Montgomery Academy High School in 1979. The summer before the season started, Alabama Assistant Coach Mal Moore called McCracken and told him that Coach Bryant wanted to see him in Bryant's office.

"I was scared to death," McCracken recalls.

"Bryant sat me down and told me, 'Take those kids that aren't good and make them think they are good. Take the good ones and make them great. Take the great ones and control them.'"

Bryant, who always cared deeply about his players and their families, was quite interested in McCracken's success. In this, his first season, McCracken was coaching Mark Tyson, Bear Bryant's grandson.

As McCracken was leaving, Bryant lightened up and smiled. "He told me to not let anything happen to his grandson and for me to take care of him and treat him just like the other boys," McCracken recalls. "He said Mark was his fishing buddy."

McCracken took Bryant's instruction on coaching to heart. "Our meeting lasted five minutes or so," McCracken says, "but those few minutes afforded me the greatest lesson I've yet to learn as a coach. You have to deal with the regular Joe and the superstar, you have to help them learn to do the right thing at the right time; if you don't they can get you beat in a big game, they can make or break the team," McCracken says.

"As Coach Bryant said, you have to coach them all to be better than they are and treat them all fairly; not the same, perhaps, but fairly."

You show me a man who belittles another
and I will show you a man who is not a
leader; or one who is not charitable, who
has no respect for the dignity of another, is
not loyal; I will show you a man
who is not a leader.

Vince Lombardi

If you want to improve yourself,
lift up someone else.

Booker T. Washington

There is little that can stand up to a man
who can conquer himself.

Louis XIV

Worry is like a rocking chair. It will give
you something to do, but it won't get you
anywhere.

Source Unknown

Your ego should not be so connected to
your success on the job, that when your
job fails, so does your ego.

General Colin Powell

Good things do happen to good people

JOHN MOTHERSHED

John Mothershed has been a head coach at Deshler High School in Tuscumbia for nine years and has amassed an 95-22 record (82 percent).

His 1998 and 1999 teams were Class 4A state champions. Both teams went 14-1.

His 2002 team was 11-2 before losing in the quarterfinals of the playoffs. He was defensive coordinator from 1987 through 1994 and coached a state championship team in 1990, a team that went 15-0.

Mothershed, a native of the area, plans on coaching at Deshler as long as possible.

Coach Mothershed, who has won two state championships as Deshler's head coach, says the foundation for his winning path was laid when he was defensive coordinator on the 1990 state championship team coached by the legendary Tandy Geralds.

"Geralds would emphasize and re-emphasize that a coach was not there to win a popularity contest. A coach is there to exercise his best judgment and, when he does, the winning and losing will take care of themselves," says Mothershed. "You've just got to ignore the outside influences and simply do what you think is right."

"The best example I can think of in explaining Coach Gerald's philosophy happened in 1990 when we were playing T.R. Miller for the Class 4A state championship," Mothershed says.

"We were undefeated in the state championship game and we hadn't been really tested all year. At halftime we were getting beat and someone screamed at Coach Geralds from the stands, 'We figured you'd find a way to lose it!'"

Deshler played a great second half and came back to win the game and the state title. "After we won the game there was a lot of elation, with people running on the field and patting us on the back and all," Mothershed recalls.

"At some point that fan who had yelled at Coach Geralds came to congratulate him for the win. A short while later, Coach Geralds turned to me and said, 'John, don't you ever forget a person patting you on the back after the game could have been the same person who tried to stab you in the back just after the first half.'"

"Coach Geralds showed me how to handle that situation," says Mothershed. "Win or lose, you still have a job to do. It's your job to mold a player off the field as well as on."

Mothershed continues, "I try to shape and mold good people, not great players, because good things happen to good people. I'm proud of our old-fashioned values. The job is not about money. The number one priority is to create better people. Money should be secondary. It's about molding kids into better people."

In reading the lives of great men, I found
that the first victory they won was over
themselves ... self-discipline with all of
them came first.

Harry S Truman

The only discipline that lasts is
self-discipline.

Bum Phillips

When you make a mistake, there are only three things you should ever do about it: admit it, learn from it, and don't repeat it.

Bear Bryant

Winning isn't getting ahead of others, it is getting ahead of where you used to be.

Roger Staubach

Organization is a habit.

George Allen

When you're through learning, you're through

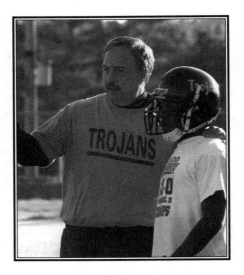

STEVE SAVARESE

Beginning in the fall of 2004, Steve Savarese will be head coach of the McGill-Toolen Yellow Jackets.

With over 30 years as a high school football coach, Savarese attributes an exceptional winning record, 262-73 (78 percent), to the relationships he has been able to develop with his players and his coaches.

Savarese spent seven years at Douglass High School in Kansas, winning a state championship in the late 1970s. He returned to Ensley High School in 1981, and, in four years, revived a strong football tradition the school had enjoyed in earlier years. From Ensley, Savarese went to Benjamin Russell in 1985, where he spent 12 years rebuilding the program.

In 1998, Savarese came to Daphne, where he won a state championship in 2001.

If you should ever have the pleasure of sitting down with **Coach Savarese** for a conversation, the first thing that will strike you is that here is a man who loves his job and attacks it with great enthusiasm for his players' education and welfare.

"There are two types of good kids on the football field," Savarese says. "There are the Petes and there are the Ralphs. The Petes are the all-American kids; everybody likes them and they make good grades. The Ralphs, on the other hand, are the uncoordinated ones. It's the mamas and daddys who like them and they make great grades," continues Savarese. "The blessing of being a high school coach is that you are responsible for instructing the Petes and the Ralphs, all of them, with the same degree of care and concern."

Savarese has coached a lot of Petes and Ralphs in his 30-year, 254-win career. "There are five Petes to 95 Ralphs," explains Savarese. "I've learned that it's usually the Ralphs who make the difference in this world. They're the ones, and not the Petes, who are more likely to give you every ounce of their effort.

"You must never, ever neglect a kid who wants to play. You can't coach a kid negatively and expect anything from him. At the end of practice, if you've jumped on a kid, especially a Ralph, you have to say something positive. The Ralphs are going to take you seriously; they're the ones who are going to improve the most and surprise the dickens out of you."

Savarese thinks the greatest trait of a true leader is humility. "Humility comes from taking risks and making mistakes," says Savarese. "Ralphs learn humility. I became a Ralph in the first game I ever coached when I made the very public mistake of crowing to my principal to 'watch out for a win' before the game even started. We got beat 40-something to nothing."

Savarese is convinced that football is not about the coaches and it's not about winning games, it's about the players—the Petes and especially the Ralphs of the world.

He who waits to do a great deal of good at once will never do anything. Life is made up of little things. True greatness consists of being great in little things.

Samuel Johnson

He who angers you defeats you.

Elizabeth Kinney

Leadership begins when we're content to
feel we're right about something
without feeling the necessity to prove
someone else wrong.

Sydney J. Harris

Temporary failure is merely an
opportunity to more intelligently
begin again.

Henry Ford

One half the troubles of this life can be
traced to saying 'Yes' too quickly and not
saying 'No' soon enough.

Josh Billings

The capacity to forgive is man's greatest attribute

JERRY DISMUKE

Jerry Dismuke, 52, a turn-around artist for over 29 years, aims to build on a proud Jess Lanier tradition established in the 1980s and 1990s, when the team was a perennial playoff contender.

Dismuke has helped to rebuild a number of football programs. In 1983, in only his second season as head coach, he took Wenonah to the quarterfinals of the state playoffs. At Dora, as offensive line coach, he assisted Joey Jones in shaping a winning program. In 1996, he took the head coaching job at Aliceville, and in 1997 the team won the Class 3A state championship.

His son, Jamarius, is a 6-5, 310 pound sophomore lineman at UAB who prepped at Parker.

"I was young, hot-headed, and eager to get after it the first day in full pads," admits **Coach Dismuke**, whose first job as head football coach was in 1982 at Wenonah High School in Birmingham.

"My ambition was to be the first black coach to win a state championship at a school with few resources and with kids who had grown up with next-to-nothing their entire lives." Dismuke had inherited a Wenonah program that had won only five games in five years. "My kids were from the projects and I was determined to show the world they could be winners, too," says Dismuke.

One of the most talented players he had inherited was Victor Morris. Morris was a 10th grader, and at 5-11, 250, he looked to be a player that could help him turn the program around. Dismuke had urged Morris to come out for off-season weight training, but Morris never showed up. When Morris, an offensive lineman, came out the first day of practice in August, Dismuke decided to ride him hard.

"I'd first make Victor go hard with his group and when he went on the blocking sled I'd make him go extra times. When he wasn't hitting the sled, I had him running laps around the field." And then tragedy struck. Victor Morris collapsed on the field.

Dismuke called the paramedics and went with him to the emergency room. "The doctors had to ice him all over his body because his temperature was so high," recalls Dismuke.

As a result of the tragedy, Morris missed his entire sophomore and half his junior year. "He was paralyzed from the waist down. It just about tore me up," Dismuke says. "If that boy had died it would have just about killed me, too."

Remarkably, Morris regained feeling in his legs and got his strength back the summer before his senior year. He came out for football and finished the season as an All-Metro lineman, winning the Most Courageous Award for the city of Birmingham. He is now a computer analyst in Birmingham and is married with a family. One of his sons plays for Wenonah.

"I thank God he recovered and came back out to play," Dismuke says. "I thank God he forgave me."

129

Find a way to make changes in yourself rather than in someone else. Most of the time, you'll find the results will be the same.

Source Unknown

God opposes the proud, but gives grace to the humble.

James Nix

Go out on the limb ... that's where the apple is.

Will Rogers

Education is the essential foundation of a strong democracy.

Barbara Bush

Excellence is the gradual result of always striving to do better.

Pat Riley

Mistakes are nothing more than important lessons in disguise

VINCE DiLORENZO

Vince DiLorenzo, now in his fourth year at Spain Park, took a young program in 2003 to the state playoffs for the first time, finishing the season with a 7-4 record and setting the stage for a strong program in the years to come.

DiLorenzo's record in 20 years as a head coach at Gadsden and Spain Park is 137-68. DiLorenzo achieved the ultimate accomplishments in high school football when he won Class 5A state championships at Gadsden High School in 1986 and 1991.

DiLorenzo lives in Hoover with his family.

"The players could have just mailed it in when we were 1-5, but they decided to work and play like winners from that Monday practice on," says **Coach DiLorenzo**, reflecting on what he considers to be the most defining moment in his head coaching career. "We challenged them and they responded to the challenge."

That Monday practice occurred in 1986, his third year as head coach of the Gadsden High School Tigers. They had struggled mightily in the first six games of the season, going 1-5. By all accounts, they were headed for what was certain to be a dismal losing season.

"I was being questioned by the fans, who weren't sure if I was the coach they thought I was," says DiLorenzo. That's when DiLorenzo and his assistants made the decision to make a stand.

They chose the Monday of the off-week after the team's fifth loss. "We decided that we were going to show the players that we had not given up," DiLorenzo said. "So we had our toughest practice all year."

DiLorenzo put his players through a three-hour workout centered on the fundamentals.

"We worked on driving the sleds, focusing on one-on-one drills and scrimmaging," he says. "We saw after that practice that our players were not going to give up. They looked at the five losses as mistakes. Everyone knows that mistakes are life's lessons in disguise."

That practice set the stage for the rest of the season. In the Tigers' next game against cross-town rival Etowah, the Tigers faced a fourth and goal at the Etowah six yard line late in the first half.

"I called the field goal team out," DiLorenzo remembers. "The players called timeout and said, 'Coach, we've got to go for it.'"

DiLorenzo saw determination in his players' eyes and reversed his decision and went for it. Quarterback David Taylor completed the touchdown pass to receiver John Massey.

The Tigers won a huge game against Etowah and never looked back, winning seven more in a row and capturing their first of two state championships under DiLorenzo.

The chains of habit are generally too small to be felt until they are too strong to be broken.

Samuel Johnson

To be wronged is nothing unless you continue to remember it.

Confucius

A public-opinion poll is no substitute for thought.

Warren Buffett

Success can lead to complacency and complacency is the greatest enemy of success.

Source Unknown

If you're too busy to help those around you succeed, you're too busy.

Source Unknown

In everything you do put God first and He
will direct you and crown your efforts
with success — *Proverbs 3:6*

SHORTY WHITE

George "Shorty" White spent 1959 through 1974 at Banks, where he took football "to another level," according to friend and fellow coach Jack Crowe, head football coach at Jacksonville State University. White won state championships at Banks in 1965, 1972, and 1973 in Class 4A, the highest classification in the state at that time. While at Banks, he posted a 100-37-3 mark for a 71 percent winning record

In 1975, White left to coach for Paul "Bear" Bryant. In 1981, White went into business as an investment adviser. He coached four more years, at Pleasant Grove High School from 1990 to 1993 and one year at American Christian Academy in Tuscaloosa, but returned to private business after that.

"Everybody needs to go through the experience of losing now and then," **Coach White** says. "When you look back at it honestly, a loss probably led you to bigger and better things."

White reflects back to the spring before the 1974 football season at Banks when he attended a Christian revival. "I had won an awful lot of football games in my life, but I still had an empty space in my heart," says White.

"I told the team that I sure wished they would come along with me," White says. "The majority of the team showed up."

At the end of his speech, the preacher asked everyone "to accept Jesus Christ as his savior." Nobody stood up and White remembers feeling awkward and uncomfortable. "Here I am, a good guy who has gone to church every Sunday. I have a happy home and good health. Do I really have to stand up and take the lead on this?"

"Thankfully," White says, "the Lord picked me up by the seat of my pants and took me down the aisle." Shortly thereafter, the Banks players, one by one, came up to declare their faith.

The Banks seniors went into the 1974 season led by nationally renowned quarterback Jeff Rutledge. After eight straight convincing wins, the pivotal game of the season was scheduled at Legion Field against undefeated Woodlawn, led by superstar running back Tony Nathan. Both teams were 8-0 and the winner was a surefire bet to win the state championship in the postseason. Banks won an extremely physical game, 18-7, playing before a crowd of 42,000, the largest ever to attend a high school game in Alabama.

"This was by far and away one of the best teams I have ever coached. When they were healthy they were unbeatable," White says. But then the injuries began. Banks had a rash of injuries the last two games of the season and couldn't overcome that obstacle in the playoffs. Homewood defeated a beaten up Banks team in the first round of the playoffs that year.

"It was, to say the least, a huge disappointment for all of us," says White. "But the faith we had in Christ and each other helped us all deal with the bitterness and the let down. Sometimes faith is firmed up when you lose something of great value," says White.

It's awfully important to win with humility. It's also important to lose with humility. I hate to lose worse than anyone, but if you never lose you won't know how to act. If you lose with humility, then you can come back.

Bear Bryant

Nothing gives a person so much advantage over another as to remain always cool and unruffled under all circumstances.

Thomas Jefferson

Good habits are as easy to form as bad
ones.

Tim McCarver

Excuses are the nails used to build a
house of failure.

Don Wilder

How a man plays the game shows
something of his character; how he loses
shows all of it.

Camden County (Georgia) Tribune

He who conquers others is strong; he who conquers himself is mighty — *Lao-tzu*

DON HANNAH

Although Don Hannah, retired, coached football for 28 years, his best years arguably were at Tarrant from 1985 to 1997. Hannah took his teams to the Class 4A quarterfinals six times and his 1988 team reached the state championship game. He won 100-plus games at Tarrant.

His 1987 team had just beaten Hewitt-Trussville 6-0 and Hannah says they were "feeling pretty good about themselves the next week." They lost to Fairfield on a Friday and Hannah had them at practice at 6:30 a.m. on the next Monday, Labor Day morning. He had them practicing until 9 a.m., then gave them a water break and worked them until 11:30. Hannah says, "Pain is temporary, but pride lasts forever."

"Discipline is not a form of punishment; discipline is a means of self-improvement," says **Coach Hannah**.

Hannah believes in discipline both on and off the football field. When one of his former players didn't demonstrate personal discipline, he focused his attentions on him and stayed on him until he respected the coach's way of doing things. "It was a challenge and a privilege for me to help them be the best they could be," says Hannah.

Hannah remembers having once spotted a potential bully in physical education class. "I was sure he had the talent to become a good football player," Hannah recalls thinking.

Hannah approached the kid and told him what he thought.

"I said, 'If you're so bad, why don't you play football? I bet you don't have the guts to do it the right way,'" says Hannah.

The kid showed up for spring practice the next year. "I worked him hard," recalls Hannah. "Some might even say I tried to run him off." The kid made it through the spring training and became the team's starting center in the fall.

"He was 6-foot-2, 190 pounds. Once, we were playing Mortimer Jordan and one of their kids spit in his face," Hannah says. The kid threw a punch back and Hannah took him out of the game. "I told him he was not going back in the game until he got himself under control and put a smile on his face. When you let someone else anger you, that person is probably going to beat you."

The player went to the locker room and came back out with three or four minutes left in the game, tapped Hannah on the shoulder and when Hannah turned around and saw him, Hannah made his decision, "The kid had a smile on his face and I sent him back in the game. He was able to finish up one of the best games of his life."

The player got a scholarship to Mississippi Valley State and, before he left school, wrote Hannah a two-page typewritten note telling the coach how much he appreciated him and his method of improvement by discipline.

The former Tarrant player still goes by to see him. "Now he gives me a hug with a smile on his face every time he sees me," Hannah laughs.

PERSEVERE

There is no limit to what a man can do or where he can go if he doesn't mind who gets the credit.

Robert Woodruff

5

When you've been going through a bad stretch, when you're struggling and the heat is on, coming at you from all quarters, sometimes you just simply have to hang in there.

The veteran coaches on these pages have each experienced at least one or two difficult seasons in their careers, times when they have done everything within their command to prepare the team, yet still found themselves having to grind through every day of the week. When the slump had finally passed, they were just thankful they had made it through yet another year.

Perseverance is the indispensable characteristic necessary to victory. It is the mainstay in every successful coach's arsenal of talents. As the saying goes, "You will often lose the battle, but can still win the war." The coaches in this chapter have certainly experienced tough times, but they have been able to work their way through challenging circumstances by pushing steadily forward, not yielding to the onslaught of adversity and conflict.

Perhaps it's true that every coach is just a play or two away from success or disappointment, but their willingness to hang in there with their kids and keep them focused at all times is what turned these coaches into true leaders.

Coaches often face difficult situations off the football field, crises they must endure and resolve in order to continue in positive directions. Whether it's a death in the family or of a friend, one of their coaches having personal problems, or one of their players in a complicated personal situation, the coach is expected to be a rock, easing the pain or finding a solution.

We learn that coaching doesn't start and end with winning and losing; it starts and ends with staying together as a team. Coaches are understandably most proud of their staffs and their players who hang in there with them, becoming better citizens and players at the end of the day. They have believed, they have planned, they have worked, and they have improved. And they have done this together as a team, as a community of players, without giving up.

5

Persistence is to the character of man as
carbon is to steel.

Napoleon Hill

Losing doesn't make me quit. It makes me
want to fight that much harder.

Bear Bryant

As long as a person doesn't admit he is defeated, he is not defeated.

Darrel Royal

You may have to fight a battle more than once to win it.

Margaret Thatcher

First, one must endure.

Ernest Hemingway

Everybody's with you when you're on top of the mountain. True friends stand beside you when you're in the valley

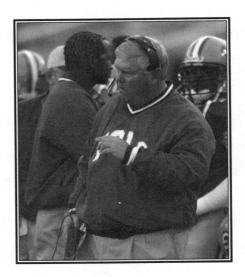

STEVE BAILEY

Steve Bailey has been at Jeff Davis for 14 of his 22 years. He has a 41-23 record and has coached a 1996 state championship team as an offensive coordinator. Bailey started out coaching at the junior high level in Montgomery and then coached one year at St. James in Montgomery.

In 2002, Bailey commandeered the Vols to an improbable run through the state playoffs, making it all the way to the championship game. This team upset three opponents, all on the road, each ranked in the top five of Class 6A.

"My most rewarding season as a head coach was in 2002," says **Coach Bailey**.

The Vols began their run for the state by first upsetting Vigor, 22-21, who had the home field advantage. They then beat Central Phenix City, 18-13. "Central Phenix City was three times better than us," says Bailey. In the state semifinals, the Vols dominated Prattville, 30-8. "It was a huge win for us," Bailey recalls.

The Vols lost to Hoover in the title game, but there's much more of the story to be told. They had achieved this remarkable string of upsets despite having faced an even more remarkable string of personal challenges over the course of the season.

"We weren't the most talented team in the state," Bailey says, "but in overcoming the trials we faced, we definitely became the closest."

First, one of Bailey's assistants was diagnosed with cancer and was placed on chemotherapy. "Our concern and prayers for him helped to pull us together," says Bailey.

Then, another coach had premature twins. There was a chance the twins wouldn't live, and if they did survive, they might face severe complications. Yet another coach was called off the field when he learned that his father had suffered a heart attack. At the hospital, the coach's mother had a heart attack in the emergency room. Finally, another coach, who was experiencing physical problems, was diagnosed with multiple sclerosis.

"Those were big tests for us," Bailey says. The Vols stayed true to their efforts and found strength. "Our coaches and players made it through, our playoff performance was superb, and we learned the value of true and lasting friendship."

The coaches' parents who were in the hospital are now doing well, and the coach with MS is taking medication that is working. "The coach with cancer is finished with his treatment and is still coaching. The twins have been released and are doing fine," says Bailey.

"The coach's *real* job," Bailey says, "is to steer young people through difficult times." In the process, perseverance builds character and the coach's job is complete.

Patience and diligence, like faith, moves mountains.

William Penn

Our greatest weakness lies in giving up. The most certain way to succeed is to always try just one more time.

Thomas A. Edison

Never discourage anyone who continually
makes progress, no matter how slow.

Plato

Something in human nature causes us
to start slacking off at our moment of
greatest accomplishment. As you become
successful, you will need a great deal of
self-discipline not to lose your sense of
balance, humility, and commitment.

Ross Perot

Tough times don't last – tough people do.

Robert Schuler

Find your strength in difficult times

MIKE BATTLES

Mike Battles has taken his teams to the playoffs in four straight years and has accumulated a record of 50-27. Battles has his football players believing that there are no limits to what they can accomplish in life.

Battles played for his father, the legendary Mike Battles Sr., at Walter Welborn High School in Anniston, where, as a junior and senior, Battles was a linebacker, punter, and place kicker for teams that reached the third round of the playoffs both years before losing to eventual Class 5A state champion Oxford.

In April of 1998, an F5 tornado with 250 mile-per-hour winds devastated the western part of Jefferson County, killing 33 people and injuring 256 more.

Oak Grove High School had been leveled and **Coach Battles**, who lived just over the hill from where the tornado had hit, killing one female student and her parents, now faced a major rebuilding effort. Battles, who was only in his second year at Oak Grove, was left to help pick up the pieces and start over. "We were a team of beaten down, discouraged football players," says Battles.

In fall 1998 the students attended Gilmore Bell High School. The football team dressed out in makeshift locker rooms in house trailers. "We became a lot closer as a team dealing with the dislocation," Battles now reflects. "We have good, hard-nosed kids who don't give up. They're not the type of kids to worry about their situation."

The coaches and players were determined to endure the circumstances. Because they had no stadium of their own, the Oak Grove team had to travel to every football game. Schools such as Briarwood Christian would let the Oak Grove team get the entire revenue from the gate.

Battles was amazed at the support from his community. "To tell you what kind of community we had, we had bigger crowds at the places we played on the road than the home team did," he says.

The determination and tenacity of the people of Oak Grove paid off when they moved into the new school in 2000. "We moved our practices to the outfield of the new baseball stadium and we found a classroom to change in. We had an entirely new football team," says Battles. "The first home game we beat Midfield 14-13. It was the first time we had beaten them in three years."

Battles and the students of Oak Grove are now in a new high school with a field house that has 80 lockers along with first-class athletic fields, including a football stadium.

Battles has his players believing they can win now because of a renewed confidence that they have overcome difficult times. They now deeply appreciate the value of hard work and the power that comes from persevering in the wake of catastrophic events.

You are never a loser until you quit trying.

Mike Ditka

It's not so important who starts the game,
but who finishes it.

John Wooden

The greatest test of courage on Earth is to bear defeat without losing heart.

Robert G. Ingersoll

No great thing is created suddenly.

Epictetus

Success seems to be largely a matter of hanging on after others have let go.

William Feather

Man's greatness can be measured by what he chooses to fight for

ROBERT MADDOX

Robert Maddox finished his 27th year as a football coach in 2003 and his second year at Auburn High School.

Maddox started as an assistant coach at Decatur High School in 1977 and 1978. He then spent 12 years at Troy State where he was on a coaching staff that won two national championships.

He was then head football coach at Valley High School, where he took two teams, his 1991 and 1992 teams, to the semifinals in Class 5A.

He then went to Gardiner Webb College in North Carolina where, as defensive coordinator, he helped lead the team to four straight winning seasons, the first time in school history.

"Kids quit in a heartbeat these days," **Coach Maddox** says, "instead of reevaluating what went wrong and sticking with it."

Maddox has worked with high school and college kids for over 27 years and has seen some significant changes that don't quite sit well with a veteran football coach.

His most recent experience of a rash of players quitting when they would have been better served by sticking it out occurred in his first season at Auburn in 2002. Maddox says they were good kids and good players who just didn't have the desire to steel themselves for the tough times.

"One thing that stands out in that first season," says Maddox, "is that the players who stayed on the job went on to win a five-overtime game against Smiths Station, and they made it to the playoffs."

Maddox is trying to build a stick-to-it attitude into his football players that they will take with them into their lives.

"If you quit in football, or at any sport for that matter, later in life you may quit on something more important like your job or even your family," he says.

Maddox says kids have come to him over the years and told him that football is hard. "I admit football is hard. I tell them, life is no rose garden, but we have it a lot better than most of the other countries in the world. Some kids take for granted how great we have it. My honest and sincere desire for my kids is to give them something they can stick with, something they can fight for. They will be better men because of it."

Maddox believes that a coach's winning percentage is a poor measure for gauging a coach's success in high school football.

"You've got to put consistent integrity in front of the kids. That's the real job, not winning and losing. You've got to show them how to do things right. Every time a kid makes a choice, you want him to be prepared to accept the consequences," says Maddox.

The consequences for quitting make it the final option. "Even if you lose, you'll learn more from losing than from quitting," says Maddox.

Act as if what you do makes a difference
and it will.

William James

Morale is a state of mind. It is
steadfastness and courage and hope.

General George Marshall

If you don't invest very much, then defeat doesn't hurt very much and winning is not very exciting.

Dick Vermeil

It takes a heck of a lot of lonely years to become an overnight success.

Source Unknown

He that can't endure the bad will not thrive to see the good.

Yiddish Proverb

There's a little boy somewhere waiting to grow up just like you

HAL RIDDLE

Hal Riddle has been a head coach for 11 years and has won a state championship at Clay-Chalkville in 1999. With an overall mark of 80-48, Riddle is entering his third season at Hewitt-Trussvile, where, as a Huskies alumnus, he will try to build on the success that Jack Wood left when he retired in 2001.

Riddle, who is a quiet leader, cites Morris Higginbotham as a tremendous mentor for him.

"He put the fear of the good Lord in you," Riddle said. "And at the same time he would lift you up. He taught you about self-discipline." That's what Riddle wants his players to take away from their experiences with him— the self discipline to give it their very best for as long as it takes to win in life.

At the beginning of the 1999 football season, **Coach Riddle** read an excerpt from a poem entitled "Little Eyes" and decided to put it on the locker room wall. "It's the kind of motivation that would show our players that their behavior on and off the field can have a huge impact on others, especially younger children," says Riddle.

There are little eyes upon you,
And they are watching night and day,
There are little ears that quickly
Take in every word you say.
You are setting an example
Every day in all you do;
For the little boy who's waiting
To grow up to be just like you.

Despite having lost three games during the regular season, the 1999 Clay-Chalkville team won the Class 6A state championship. During the playoffs, after Riddle's team had won an overtime game with Pelham, one of his players approached him on the field.

"My cornerback Chris Walker walked over to me and said, 'Coach, a little kid who was watching the game came up to me and wanted my chin strap and my wrist band,'" Riddle recalls. Walker told Riddle that he now really understood what that simple poem meant. "Walker said to me, 'Coach, you're right, they are watching us,'" remembers Riddle. "That brought it home to him."

Riddle forged a team that shared a commitment to hard work and an ability to persevere through tough times in the season. Three loses didn't break them; they were strong enough to come together to win it all at the end. Riddle understood the pulse of his team and knew they were special. And he knew how to motivate them.

The simple words in a simple poem affected his players, and at least one of his players learned that actions really do make a difference in a younger person's life.

Go the extra mile. It's never crowded.

Source Unknown

Great works are performed, not by
strength, but by perseverance.

Samuel Johnson

He never knew when he was whipped …
so he never was.

Louis L'Amour

If you get knocked down, get up.

Bear Bryant

In any contest between power and
patience, bet on patience.

W.B. Prescott

Winners won't win all of the time, but it's
a safe bet that quitters won't win at all

RONNY MASSEY

Ronny Massey, head coach for 26 years, has posted a 179-75 record (70 percent). In the many years he has coached football, he has suffered only three losing seasons.

When Massey took over at Citronelle in 1982, the team had only one winning season in 12 years prior. When Massey took over at Grissom in 1999, the school had only one winning season in the 17 years before that.

Massey emphasizes staying focused and determined whenever a player puts on the uniform.

Coach Massey and his Grissom team came to Birmingham three weekends in a row for the year 2000 state playoffs. On the first weekend, the Tigers beat Huffman, which was 11-0 at the time, in the second round. Next, they defeated Clay-Chalkville, the defending state champion in Class 6A, in the last minute of the quarterfinals. Although they lost to eventual state champion Hoover in the semifinals, it was indeed a "winning" year.

Massey had three players in the 2000 season who stood out because of their relentless desire to win. "These guys just were not going to let up," says Massey.

Jayson Swain, who played for Massey from 1999 to 2002, was perhaps the most talented player Massey has ever coached. In 2000, his sophomore year, Swain, who ran a 4.41 40-yard dash, caught 94 passes for 1,125 yards and 17 touchdowns as a wide receiver. Swain became a wide receiver for Tennessee.

Roy Mitros was the middle linebacker for the 2000 team. In a game against Butler, Mitros came up huge. Kenneth Darby, now a tailback with Alabama, tried to dive over the top of the line for the game-winning score, but Mitros met him head-on and knocked the ball loose. Grissom recovered the fumble to preserve the victory.

"I had to watch out for him," Massey says of Mitros. "He didn't know how to gear down; he was such a total warrior." Mitros joined the Marines, serving with the 4th Infantry Division that went into Baghdad in 2003.

Tyler Weaver was Massey's quarterback. In 2000, Weaver threw for 2,307 yards, completing 179 of 307 passes with 32 touchdowns. In the 2000 quarterfinals against Clay-Chalkville he brought the team back in the last minute, driving them from their own 30 to win the game on a 15-yard touchdown pass with less than 10 seconds left. Clay had gone ahead with a touchdown with a minute left. On the Grissom ensuing possession, Weaver came back to the huddle and told his offensive teammates with certainty that Clay-Chalkville had made a bad mistake—they had "left too much time on the scoreboard."

"These boys were nothing but total winners, who showed what it means to hang tough in the face of fire."

Big shots are only little shots who kept on shooting.

Harvey Mackay

Some days you are the dog, some days you are the hydrant.

Source Unknown

Be true to your work, your word, and your friend.

Henry David Thoreau

Success consists of getting up just one more time than you fall.

Oliver Goldsmith

Be like a postage stamp: Stick to one thing till you get there.

Josh Billings

Become an example so that others may follow

LOUIS WHITE

Louis White coached 30 years in the high school ranks, 27 of those years as head coach at Courtland, where he developed championship football teams in Class 1A.

White started at Courtland in 1970, and his first team went 0-9. He won three games in 1971, four in 1972 and six in 1973. His teams kept getting better and better because of their coach's uncompromising desire to excel and fierce dedication to the school.

His overall record is 186-76 (71 percent) and he took 17 of his teams to the playoffs and won four state championships in 1988, 1989, and 1990, and again in 1995. The Chiefs were runners-up in 1991.

Coach White was tough on his players, and they responded with a tenacious attitude, developing an understanding of the true rewards that come with staying at a task and not quitting until the day is done.

Each year, White drove his seniors to take leadership roles on the team and convinced them to buy into his program. It became their job, not his, to sell the virtues of tenacity and determination to the younger players.

"I constantly put pressure on the older guys to step out front and take charge," White said. "They were terrific guys who would come to you before the games and say, 'Don't worry coach. We got this one.' They had confidence in themselves. Losing was nowhere in their minds."

White said that if a player was skipping school or trying to get out of practice, the older guys would go find him and make him practice. The players also responded to White's emphasis on academics. "They knew what they had to do to enable them to play football and they made school a priority," says White.

White said that many of his players went on to serve in the military and told him that basic training was a breeze compared to Courtland's practices.

"I wanted them to go out and be successful and not to give up," White says.

White saw the work ethic on the field carrying over into the classroom and into the player's future lives. "I wanted them to be tough enough to hang in and do what they had to do to take care of their family," White says. "I wanted them to be good citizens and do something for society."

White says the best part of his job was his relationship with his players.

"I was so close to them," he says. "The guys would do anything to not let you down. They would give me all they had."

And they excelled.

Character consists of what you do on the
third and fourth tries.

James A. Michener

Be more concerned with your character
than your reputation, because your
character is what you really are, while
your reputation is merely what others
think you are.

John Wooden

Defeat never comes to any man until he admits it.

Josephus Daniels

Energy and persistence conquer all things.

Benjamin Franklin

Never give in. Never give in. Never, never, never—in nothing great or small, large or petty—never give in except to conviction of honor and good sense. Never yield to force; never yield to the apparently overwhelming might of the enemy ...

Winston Churchill, October 29, 1941

169

You will most likely become what you think about all day long

BILL SPARKS

Bill Sparks, retired, served 40 years and six months in the Birmingham school system. He was a football coach at Midfield High School from 1975 to 1991, accruing a record of 136-73-2 and taking his team to the semifinals in 1981. He took six teams to the playoffs.

He also was a baseball coach at Ensley and at Midfield where he earned a 327-120 record with a state championship in 1988. He coached 125 young men who received an athletic scholarship, and 30 of his players are in teaching and coaching.

He was instrumental in making Midfield among the first schools in the United States to implement a mandatory drug testing program for all athletes. He also was the leader in building a 5,000-square-foot field house at Midfield, which is now named Bill Sparks Field House.

In 40 years of teaching and coaching, **Coach Sparks** taught and lived class and had a genuine love for his players. Most of his players gave Sparks everything they had because of a respect and mutual affection for their coach.

One of Sparks' favorite football players was Shoney Young who played for him at Midfield High School in 1978 and 1979. Young was an offensive tackle who was an All-County player his senior season.

In a thrilling three-overtime win over Dora, Midfield ran a 25-power pass running directly behind Young's block leading to the game winning score. At school, Sparks hired Young to do maintenance work after he got out at 1 p.m. to enable Young to get through high school financially.

Sparks said that Young's work ethic and determination on the football field was one of the keys to his success as a player.

"He gave you everything he had," Sparks said. "He was a very serious player who stayed after practice. After we did our running he would go hit the sled. He would do the extra things to make himself a better ball player."

And he was a very likeable young man, according to Sparks. "If you met him you would like him in five minutes."

Young is now in Portland, Oregon, working for Nike. Nike is paying him to leave work at 3 p.m. and serve as a volunteer assistant football coach for a school of economically deprived students.

"We talk every three months," Sparks said. "He says I'm the daddy he never had."

When you give a kid everything you've got, most of the time he will respond.

That's how Bill Sparks touched so many players in his community who still talk to him today. The friendship that Sparks and Young have is for life.

To Sparks, that was and still is the most satisfying part of his teaching and coaching career.

AFTERWARDS

When the one great scorer comes to write against your name, He marks not that you won or lost, but how you played the game.

Grantland Rice

6

Great coaches are great mentors.

Their objective may be to prepare young men to play football, but their ambition is to teach these same young men that there is more to life than just football. In the pecking order of importance, football comes behind faith in God, family and community, and education.

Alabama high school coaches work tirelessly throughout the year to instill valuable life lessons. They enjoy coaching young people, there is no doubt about that; but, as Briarwood Christian Coach Fred Yancey and Trinity Coach Randy Ragsdale have said, "Football is a great game, but a terrible God."

Even though they are single-minded in their focus on the football field, coaches are acutely aware that their players need support and encouragement off the field as well. Their players, after all, are in school, and the opportunity to go to college is very important to each of them. Some athletes will receive football scholarships, and they have to make the mandatory grades and test scores to qualify for college. The majority of the other players, however, will not get football scholarships and they must strive to get into college on their own educational and extracurricular achievements.

These coaches understand and stress the importance of studying, learning, and progressing in the classroom. And there are other things these coaches emphasize: being with a secure family, spending time with friends, and enjoying life. The things in life that matter.

Coaches are there for the kids to teach them values and help them become better, more productive people: Attention in the classroom, punctuality at school and at practice, respect for parents and adults, and trust and concern for teammates and classmates. There is great intrinsic value in the coach's instruction.

No doubt the game is important to the coaches, but, in truth, they are there to make their players better people. When they get their players together before a practice they talk about life along with football. They train their young men to understand valuable lessons needed when facing the real world's opportunities and obstacles.

In the end, the great coach teaches a player how to win and to lose, how to give and to take—in short, how to lead a balanced life.

It is not how much we have, but how much we enjoy that makes happiness. It is not how much we win but how much we enjoy playing that makes for victory.

Charles H. Spurgeon

There are only two ways to live your life: one, as though nothing is a miracle, the other is as though everything is a miracle.

Albert Einstein

The true measure of a man is how
he treats someone who can do him
absolutely no good.

Samuel Johnson

There are two types of people – those who
come into a room and say, "Well, here I
am!" and those who come in and say, "Ah,
there you are."

Frederick L. Collins

Individual commitment to a group
effort – that is what makes a team work,
a company work, a society work, a
civilization work.

Vince Lombardi

It's just a football game

FRED YANCEY

In his 15 years at Briarwood and over the course of his 35 years overall as a coach, Fred Yancey has brought out the very best in his football players. In 1998 and 1999 his Lions teams were state champions in Class 3A and in 2003 his team won the 5A state title. His teams have been to the state championship semifinals on three other occasions.

The Lions have made the playoffs a remarkable 12 consecutive years. They repeated as region champions for 10 consecutive years. Their 2002 loss to Jess Lanier was their first regional loss since 1994. Since 1996, Briarwood has a 100-12 record (89 percent). Yancey's Coaching record is 180-62-1 (74 percent).

Even though he has enjoyed considerable success on the football field, **Coach Yancey** most highly prizes his relationships with his players. He relishes his role as a teacher and as a spiritual mentor.

Former Briarwood assistant coach Jay Mathews, who is now a head football coach in Tennessee, coached with Yancey for over 13 years. Few could possibly know Yancey's coaching style as well as he does.

"Results are what count with Coach Yancey," says Mathews, "and he's not going to boast about his accomplishments even though he has, by anyone's standards, quite a few."

What Mathews says counts and carries a great deal of weight to those who follow the Briarwood program.

Mathews' quarterbacks threw for a remarkable 20,000 yards, leading to 206 touchdowns in 13 seasons. Mathews coached Tim Castille, now a sophomore on the University of Alabama Football team, who gained 9,554 all-purpose yards, a state record, and scored 102 touchdowns in his Briarwood career, with 17 of them coming from more than 50 yards out.

"It is so hard to quote Coach Yancey because what stands out about him is his life not his words," Mathews says.

"One of the things he always asks us to do at the end of every practice or game is to come together and hold our team prayer, win or lose, happy or sad. A key point Coach Yancey emphasizes can be summed up in the saying 'Big team, little me.'

"He is always prompting the players to commit to a larger process," says Mathews. "Yancey is a master team builder, and he personifies the saying that actions speak louder than words.

"One year we ran a fake punt with our punter backed up to the 12 yard line. I wasn't sure if it was the right call with us being so far back on our side of the field," says Mathews. "We scored an 81 yard touchdown. I said to him, 'What a gutsy call.'

"All Coach Yancey said was, 'It's just a football game.'"

Never complain, never explain.

Benjamin Disraeli

To know when you have enough is to be rich.

Lao-tzu

Not only must we be good, but we also
must be good for something.

Henry David Thoreau

You never know how a horse will pull until
you hook it to a heavy load.

Bear Bryant

One man practicing sportsmanship is far
better than a hundred teaching it.

Knute Rockne

Never ask 'What have you done for me lately'

RICKEY JOHNSON

Rickey Johnson began his career at Mount Hope High School, coaching for three years, then spent five years at Hatton before moving on to coach at Hazlewood in 1986.

Johnson is now back at his hometown school, Hatton, after spending 13 terrific seasons at Hazlewood. He has won 178 games in his 26 years as head coach.

He won Class 2A state championships in 1990, 1991, and 1992, and he won a Class 1A state crown in 2000. He also won two state championships as an assistant coach at Hazlewood in 1988 and 1989. His 1993 team was a runner-up, and so was his 1995 team.

Coach Johnson has experienced many difficult situations in the coaching arena.

Despite taking eight Hazlewood teams to the state finals and winning six state titles as a head coach or as an assistant, he will tell you that, as a coach, he continually felt the intense pressure that the fans put on him and his players. Fans who've been spoiled by a successful program often exhibit, according to Johnson, what he calls a "what have you done for me lately" attitude.

In 1994, Johnson's Hazlewood team entered its annual match up with Hatton, having beaten Hatton for 19 straight years up to that time. But this game would go to Hatton and would be memorable to Johnson for a number of reasons besides the loss.

Hatton intercepted Hazlewood's quarterback "three or four times" Johnson remembers. Johnson explains that the Hazlewood-Hatton rivalry was deep and the fans got riled up at the unexpected loss. Many of them turned their anger on the young Hazlewood quarterback, Johnson recalls.

Hazlewood's quarterback lived in the projects. When Johnson drove him home after the game "people were shouting at him, calling him a sellout," Johnson says.

The Monday night after the game, Johnson invited the boy over to his house and cooked him a steak, hoping it would make him feel better about himself and give him support. The boy, who never had much, told Johnson that "this was as good as lunchroom food."

"A lot of people would take that as criticism," Johnson says, "but I knew he meant it as a good thing."

Johnson is convinced that when you show your kids you care about them and make them feel special they will respond in a positive way and give you their very best.

"Anybody who says they don't care about what the fans think is not shooting straight with you," says Johnson. "I've been in situations where I knew the kids' families and I've been in situations where I didn't. Even though it bothers you a little more when you know the kids' families," says Johnson, "either way it bothers you."

181

It's not where you begin, it's where you end up.

Source Unknown

Life is like a dog sled team. If you ain't the lead dog, the scenery never changes.

Lewis Grizzard

If you don't run your own life, somebody else will.

John Atkinson

It is not the critic who counts; not the man who points out how the strong man stumbles or where the doer of deeds could have done better. The credit belongs to the man who is actually in the arena, whose face is marred by dust and sweat and blood, who strives valiantly, who errs and comes up short again and again, because there is no effort without error or shortcoming, but who knows the great enthusiasms, the great devotions, who spends himself for a worthy cause; who, at the best, knows, in the end, the triumph of high achievement, and who, at the worst, if he fails, at least he fails while daring greatly, so that his place shall never be with those cold and timid souls who knew neither victory nor defeat.

Theodore Roosevelt

If you can shake the hand of the man who
just beat you, you both walk away a winner

BOB NEWTON

*Bob Newton has set the standard for excellence at Homewood, where he
has won state championships in 1995, his first year, in 2000, and in 2002.
He took his 2001 team to the 5A state championship game also. Newton's
overall record is 95-23.*

*Newton played high school football at Russellville where he and his
teammates won state titles in 1967 and 1968. He played on the offensive
line. He played college football at Samford and was part of a team that
won the Division II National Championship. He gets the most out of his
teams and the results speak for themselves.*

Coach Newton emphasizes sportsmanship both during and after football games. "You do the best you can and that's all you can do, and then, whether you win or lose," says Newton "you shake the other man's hand."

The Patriots have had a storied rivalry with the Briarwood Christian Lions over the past few years, with each team beating the other in big games. In 2002, the Lions beat the Patriots during the regular season, but then the Patriots beat the Lions in the semifinals of the playoffs. In 2003 the Patriots defeated the Lions in the regular season, but this time the Lions came back and won in the semifinals. Both the 2002 Homewood team and the 2003 Briarwood Christian team went on to win the respective year's state championship.

"Both teams showed class during and after each game," Newton says. "Neither one of us liked it but both teams behaved and handled it like they're supposed to. Each team told the other good luck and there were no hard feelings. That's what we try to tell our players all the time."

Newton had a roughly similar experience with Benjamin Russell out of Alexander City. Newton's team lost to Benjamin Russell in 1999 in the playoffs and then went on to beat them in the 2000 state championship.

"Both situations were similar," Newton said. "Both coaching staffs and teams handled it with class."

After Homewood won the remarkable five-overtime game against Benjamin Russell in the 2000 state championship game, Newton went down to Alexander City the following week to talk to the Benjamin Russell players. He told them there were no losers in that game and he was confident that their team would be back.

And the next year, 2001, although Homewood won the regular season match-up, Benjamin Russell would go on to take the state title in the championship game.

"We tell our players to handle winning and losing the same way," says Newton. "Go up to your opponent and shake his hand, look him in the eye, and tell him good game, then go about your business."

Many persons have a wrong idea of what constitutes true happiness. It is not attained through self-gratification but through fidelity to a worthy purpose.

Helen Keller

We need to learn to set our course by the stars, not by the lights of every passing ship.

General Omar N. Bradley

A leader who keeps his ear to the ground
allows his rear end to become a target.

Source Unknown

We didn't all come over in the same ship,
but we're all in the same boat.

Bernard M. Baruch

Courage is contagious.

Billy Graham

Football's about the kids and not about the score

CHARLIE HEARN

Charlie Hearn coached high school football for 39 years and accumulated a 289-106 record (73 percent). He won state championships in 1961 at Crossville and in 1971 at Tarrant. He also started football at Erwin, and he coached at Hueytown, Valley Head, and Etowah, among other schools.

He was selected coach of the year in the state twice and had four undefeated teams. He coached four high school All-America's and several players who were all-state. He had 11 boys play for him who became ministers. He retired in 1992.

Coach Hearn attributes his longevity as a successful 39-year high school football coaching veteran to a promise he made when he was 16 years old.

Hearn was driving a truck for his dad, carrying chert, a type of soil and gravel used as the foundation material for sidewalks and highways. According to Hearn, he had the truck loaded too heavily, and, as he was guiding the truck up a mountain road, the truck stalled out. When he put on the brakes, the front end started to come off the ground; he threw it in reverse and let out the clutch. Sure enough, the front end came down, but the truck was now headed backward down the mountain.

There was a bluff to Hearn's right and a ditch to his left. "I was trying to guide it to the ditch," Hearn recalls. "I realized that I couldn't make it and I opened the door to jump out." Before he could, however, the truck went off the bluff and turned over, stopping 40 feet below.

When he came to, he turned his head to the right and his ear hit him in the mouth. "I realized I was in bad shape and I started hollering," he says. He would yell until his mouth got dry.

Two brothers who were plowing on the side of the mountain heard him; one brother scrambled down the bluff to help Hearn and the other went for help.

Hearn had lost a lot of blood. "I knew the only way I was going to live was through God's help," he says. "So I promised God that if He would let me live that I would do my best to serve Him in whatever capacity that He led me to."

It took 16 men to pick up the truck off Hearn. He had 17 broken bones and his right ear was cut off. A doctor in Gadsden was able to sew his ear back on, but he stayed on his back for over 10 weeks.

Years later, he remembers the power of that promise and now he says with great certainty, "Football's about the kids not about the score."

A promise kept.

When you get to where you're going, the
first thing to do is to take care of the horse
that got you there.

Unknown

Do something for somebody every day for
which you do not get paid.

Albert Schweitzer

You can tell more about a person by what he says about others than you can about what others say about him.

Leo Aikman

There are two things to aim at in life. First, to get what you want and after that to enjoy it. Only the wisest of mankind achieve the second.

Logan Pearsall Smith

He that wrestles with us, strengthens our nerves and sharpens our skills. Our antagonist is our helper.

Edmund Burke

Let the other guy lose his cool

RANDY RAGSDALE

Randy Ragsdale, a coach for 25 years, has earned a great deal of respect not only for his record as a head coach, 137-39 (78 percent), but also for the way he emphasizes sportsmanship and class on the field.

Ragsdale has spent the last 15 years at Trinity Presbyterian in Montgomery. He led his team to the Class 4A semifinals in the school's first year in Class 4A, in 2000. In 2001, 2002, and 2003 Trinity finished each regular season undefeated. They went 15-0 in 2003 and defeated Deshler at Legion Field to win the Class 4A state championship.

While his practices are demanding, they are never over one hour and 45 minutes, allowing his players to get home, be with their families and get their homework done.

Coach Ragsdale's father never told him or his younger brother, Scott, what to do. "Dad would advise us on the consequences of our actions then would let each of us decide what we thought was the right thing to do," Ragsdale recalls.

Randolph Sr. was a coach for over 12 years and then became a salesman for a company that two men he knew had started. Ragsdale says his dad was the consummate professional salesman, looking people in the eye when he shook hands, always honest, never telling them what they wanted to hear just to get the sale.

"He was also passionate about his sons and their sports," Ragsdale says, smiling. "Even though he had been a coach, he would never try to interfere with any of our coaches. The only time he would step in and speak up during a sports event was if he felt a player's physical well-being was in danger."

One such instance stands out in Ragsdale's mind. "I was wrestling for Rockdale High School in Georgia. We were wrestling the best team in the state and it got down to my match in the heavyweight division," Ragsdale remembers. "This guy was 6-foot-3, the strongest guy I ever fought in my life."

The two wrestled to a stalemate in the first two periods and were tied 0-0 at the end of the third.

"The crowd was electric," Ragsdale said. "I remember shooting for his legs right as the referee blew the whistle at the end of the third period. I stood up and he slugged me with his forearm right in my face. I fell to the floor in shock."

Ragsdale's team got the penalty point and won the match. That's when tempers started heating up.

"The ref lost control of the mat and the teams started yelling at each other," Ragsdale says. "My daddy came down and he and the ref restored order. He had coached the ref when he was younger. They both knew that something bad was about ready to happen."

Ragsdale learned a lot from his father about personal courage and an unyielding desire to do the right thing and live with the decision. It was one of his father's lessons he has never forgotten.

193

The fellow who does things that count
doesn't usually stop to count them.

Source Unknown

You will find as you look back upon your
life that the moments that stand out are
the moments when you have done things
for others.

Henry Drummond

194

Success has nothing to do with what you gain in life or accomplish for yourself. It's what you do for others.

Danny Thomas

The great use of life is to spend it for something which may outlast it.

William James

To know what needs to be done, and then to do it, comprises the whole philosophy of practical life.

William Osler

Always count on the man who won't be counted out

BUDDY ANDERSON

Buddy Anderson has spent his entire 32-year career as a football coach at Vestavia Hills High School. He has been head football coach and athletics director for 26 of those years. He has been one of the most successful coaches in the state over the last four decades posting a 218-93 record (70 percent).

He has won Class 6A state championships in 1980 and 1998. He has been voted state coach of the year three times. The athletic teams under his watch as athletics director have won 43 state titles. He was inducted into the 2003 Alabama High School Hall of Fame.

In his 32 years of coaching football at Vestavia Hills High School, **Coach Anderson** has had many great young men come through his program, but perhaps his greatest inspiration came from Robbie Rookis, whose older brother, Ricky, also played for Anderson.

"After playing football in the seventh grade, Robbie was diagnosed with leukemia," recalls Anderson. "He weighed 150 in the seventh grade but because of radiation treatments he was down to 100 pounds when I met him," says Anderson.

Anderson remembers holding a Fellowship of Christian Athletes meeting at his house that year. The group of players said a prayer for Robbie, who, with his parents, was at the meeting.

"Robbie stood up and prayed out loud saying, 'Thank you, Lord, for my friends, that they care about me so much,'" Anderson recalls. "From that point on Robbie started getting better."

In eighth grade Robbie went through two-a-day practices. "He wanted to be a part of the team badly," says Anderson. After playing in a game early in the season, he went back to Memphis for treatment and returned to the playing field at the end of the season. He played one down at wide receiver.

In the ninth grade, Robbie had gotten better through treatment. At this point, according to Anderson, he had an 80 percent chance of surviving. He started on the offensive and defensive lines for the freshman team. During his sophomore year, Vestavia was 0-7. Robbie did get in some playing time. "Robbie's positive attitude started to truly motivate me," Anderson now recalls. "We were struggling, but Robbie helped me settle down and keep the season in perspective when he said to me one day, 'Coach, it'll all work out.'" After Vestavia beat Bradshaw in the eighth game, Robbie said to Anderson with his arm around him, "Coach I told you we were going to do it."

"He ended up playing all through high school and graduating and going to college, where he worked hard and did well," Anderson says. "He's married and doing well in business today. His teammates could always count on him. He was, and continues to be, a real inspiration to all of us."

When nobody around you seems to
measure up, it's time to check your
yardstick.

Bill Lemley

Sports do not build character.
They reveal it.

Heywood Hale Broun

We make a living by what we get, we make
a life by what we give.

Sir Winston Churchill

Never trouble another for what you can do
for yourself.

Thomas Jefferson

Confidence doesn't come out of nowhere.
It's a result of something ... hours and days
and weeks and years of constant work and
dedication.

Roger Staubach

Every time someone challenges you,
you're offered an unparalleled opportunity

PERRY SWINDALL

In 1998, Perry Swindall moved to Russellville, where his record is 62-16. He has back-to-back Class 5A state championship game appearances in 2002 and 2003, and has reached the state finals six times as a coach.

Swindall, whose overall coaching record is 141-48 (75 percent), started as strength coach and defensive line coach at Marion Military Institute and then became defensive coordinator at Oneonta High School. In 1989 Swindall got the job as head coach at Daleville High School. Swindall's record at Daleville was 79-32 from 1989 to 1997. He won the Class 4A state title in 1992 and was runner-up in 1993.

Coach Swindall saw a lot of success as an assistant head coach at Oneonta, where his teams went 58-8 in five years. And Swindall saw a lot of success as a defensive coordinator at Marion Military Institute, where his team went 8-2 in one year.

When he was offered the head coaching job at Daleville High School, in southeast Alabama, and accepted, he knew it would be a major rebuilding project.

His team went 2-8 the first year.

The next spring after the rocky start, he got a call from Coach Wayne Woodham of Eufaula, who wanted to scrimmage Swindall's team.

Woodham had called Swindall in March and they had tentatively agreed to set up a scrimmage for spring training in April or May. However, Swindall didn't hear from Woodham in April, so he thought perhaps there was not going to be a scrimmage.

Swindall started spring training on April 25. Then he got a call.

"Woodham said he wanted to scrimmage on May 14," recalls Swindall, "and he began setting down all the rules."

Swindall knew that his 4A team stood a good chance of getting killed by Woodham's team, which was a perennial state title contender in Class 5A. Woodham had won a state championship when he was coaching at Greenville.

"I thought we were going to get embarrassed. Eufaula had 85 players and we had only 35 or 40," Swindall says. "I thought we might get some kids hurt, so I tried to beg out of it. Coach Woodham told me to stop crying and start working."

Swindall received a jolt from that comment. In very short order, he prepared his team thoroughly for the scrimmage. Daleville only lost 7-6 and the junior varsity team won 14-7. That year Daleville won 11 games. The next year Daleville won nine games and the following year they won the state championship.

"After I got challenged I worked harder than I've ever worked," Swindall says.

"Those 10th graders won the state championship in two years. That was a proud moment in Daleville and it was all on account of that challenge by Coach Woodham."

Be kind, for everyone you meet is fighting
a hard battle.

Plato

Every life has its dark and cheerful hours.
Happiness comes from choosing which to
remember.

Source Unknown

It's amazing how many people beat you at golf once you're no longer president.

George H. W. Bush

To laugh often and much, to win the respect of intelligent people, and the affection of children, to earn the appreciation of honest critics and endure the betrayal of false friends, to appreciate beauty, to find the best in others, to leave the world a bit better, whether by a healthy child, a garden patch, or a redeemed social condition, to know that even one life has breathed easier because you have lived, this is to have succeeded.

Ralph Waldo Emerson.

It ain't over till it's over.

Yogi Berra

Show genuine interest in the lives of everyone you meet

LARRY BOYKIN

Larry Boykin has compiled a 85-37 record on the football field over the last 10 years for Southern Choctaw in southwestern Alabama. His teams won Class 2A state titles in 1998, 1999 and 2002 .

Boykin took a program that finished 1-8 in 1995, and, by 1998, had won the state championship. Boykin stresses discipline on the field and in the classroom. Boykin checks every one of his kids' report cards and stresses the work ethic in the classroom. Boykin, who celebrates his 25th year as a coach and 10th as Southern Choctaw head coach, says his tried-and-true formula for winning at every level is to be unequivocally interested in the lives of the people around you. "That takes care of everything else," says Boykin, "including winning football games."

Vince Lombardi once said, "It's easy to have faith in yourself when you're number one. What you got to have is faith when you're not yet a winner." **Coach Boykin** has one of the elite programs in the state as his teams have won three Class 2A state championships in five years. But it wasn't that way in Boykin's first four years on the job.

Boykin, who takes an interest in his players in school just as much as he does on the football field, took over for the Indians in 1994. He led his team to the second round of the Class 3A playoffs where they lost to Luverne, a team that went on to win the state. In 1995 his team had two seniors, two juniors, five sophomores, 11 freshmen and two eighth graders and moved down to Class 2A. With a tough schedule featuring the likes of UMS Wright (4A), St. Paul's (5A) and Thomasville (4A) the Indians struggled through a 1-8 season.

"Those ninth graders believed they would win if they would stick through it," Boykin said.

In 1996 the team finished 3-7. During that season, Ron Ingram, high school editor for The Birmingham News, told Boykin that by the time his sophomores were seniors he expected to see them in Birmingham.

In 1997 the Indians had another tough schedule and finished the season at 5-6, losing to Cordova in the first round of the playoffs.

"After that game it was like a funeral home in the locker room. Everybody was crying," Boykin remembers. "I didn't say anything and told them to take two weeks off, go home and study, and be ready for winter workouts after the Christmas Holidays. Nearly 17 players were in the weight room and running the next Monday."

Boykin recalls "that all the team talked about was going 15-0." Boykin says that most of the fans thought it was a joke, but the players "went out and did exactly that."

Those seniors, who were freshmen in 1995, won it all in 1998 and laid the foundation for a dominant program in Class 2A. "It's good people caring about each other and doing the right thing. That's the essence of success."

ACKNOWLEDGMENTS

I wish I could have included every one of the coaches I have followed over my many years as a sportswriter. Our children are in good hands as we give them over to coaches who have consistently proven themselves to be terrific men and women, good souls and shining examples for us all.

I must thank, in particular, Joey Jones, Vince DiLorenzo, and Bob Newton. Before I decided to move forward with my plans for this book, these guys gave me a critical heads up on what to expect while interviewing other coaches around the state. Their unqualified enthusiasm for the project and all that it represents motivated me to make this project the very best it could be.

My Powerade buddies at Coca-Cola, Claude Nielsen, Thacher Worthen, Mike Suco, Chip Sutter, and Craig Samples, shared in my vision for the book. Our meetings together were always fun, informative, and productive. They made this book the real thing.

Much of the credit for the editorial development of this project goes to Dan Washburn, Executive Director of the Alabama High School Athletics Association, and his colleague Joe Evans, both of whom primed the pump with good, sound advice as I started off on my interview quest.

I owe a special debt of gratitude to Bob Farley of the Post-Herald and Bill Segrest of HKW Associates, both of whom brought their considerable knowledge of design and technology (as well as an unbeatable work ethic) to bear on achieving a great look for the book's layout and the pictures of the coaches featured.

Melanie McCraney and John Bagby of McCraney Public Relations provided their significant marketing talents to make this project a success. Their knowledge of Alabama business, generally, and in school fundraising, particularly, was an immense benefit in giving this project a respectable chance in a busy world. Additionally, they had the good judgment to introduce the project to Iris Thorpe and Tommy Brigham, each of whom has had a great deal of experience as parents of high school athletes. Iris Thorpe's insights into a typical booster club's activities lead us all to a better understanding of the way high school moms of football players think and care about the boys on the field.

There are a host of others, including Jim & Goodloe White, Kealon Drake, Elizabeth Drennen, Clyde Anderson, Sheldon Webster, Charlie Haines, Leslie Kelly, Josh Lancaster, Clay Ragsdale, Kathy Sheffield, Erica Dowdle, and Marjorie White, who generously offered their time and their support during the developmental stages of this work. The power of their belief in the message of this book was a kindness that will always be remembered.

Finally, I'd like to thank my editor and good friend, Bobby Frese, for the numerous hours he spent organizing my work, strengthening my writing and offering his counsel. This project could not have been produced without his guidance and absolute belief in the subject matter.

David White
Birmingham, Alabama
July 12, 2004

Index – By Coach

Index – By High School